IF IT DOESN'T PAN OUT

Barbara Bloch

IF IT DOESN'T PAN OUT

HOW TO COPE WITH COOKING DISASTERS

D E M B N E R B O O K S

New York

Dembner Books
Published by Red Dembner Enterprises Corp. 1841 Broadway,
New York, N.Y. 10023
Distributed by W.W. Norton & Company, Inc. 500 Fifth Avenue,
New York, N.Y. 10110

Library of Congress Cataloging in Publication Data

Bloch, Barbara.
    If it doesn't pan out.

    Includes index.
    1. Cookery.   I. Title.   II. Title: How to cope with cooking disasters.
TX652.B584   641.5   80-26508
ISBN 0-934878-02-1

This book is dedicated, with pride and delight,
to four very special young women—
my daughters Beth, Ellen, Phyllis, and Jill.
Fine cooks, and thoroughly confident in the kitchen,
they have given me endless satisfaction
by their interest in and appreciation of
good food, lovingly prepared.

Acknowledgement

To Rita Barrett, my good friend and associate, special thanks are owed for invaluable assistance and support. Her splendid knowledge of cooking and her research capabilities, coupled with an unfailing sense of humor, were essential ingredients in the development of this book.

CONTENTS

IF IT DOESN'T PAN OUT

INTRODUCTION

If you've never had a failure,
you've never cooked.

We can all be reassured about cooking disasters by remembering the down-to-earth advice of Julia Child. During one of her early television shows, she was busily flipping potato pancakes when one of them landed on the stove instead of in the pan. She picked it up calmly, brushed it off, and went right on with the show. Looking directly into the camera, she said, with great aplomb: "Remember, you are alone in the kitchen."

Even the most knowledgeable and experienced cooks have an occasional failure, although some may not always be willing to admit it. You probably have had yours, too. But whether you're on television, alone in the kitchen, or cooking with the help of family and friends, there are ways you can cope with many cooking disasters, and this book is filled with solutions that will work.

Kitchen disasters fall into different categories.

Some can be corrected. IF IT DOESN'T PAN OUT tells you how to repair dishes so you can serve what you started to make in the first place.

Some can be rescued by turning the dish into something quite different from what you originally intended. IF IT DOESN'T PAN OUT is filled with reliable, tested suggestions—ideas that work—for achieving that kind of magic.

Alas, some failures just can't be saved. There is simply nothing to do except shrug your shoulders and start cooking again. To help you overcome that kind of disaster, this book contains simple, quick, but elegant recipes for company fare, made from ingredients that can be stored easily and safely for just such emergencies.

But in each case—from the mild disappointment to the into-the-garbage-with-it failure—it is important to understand what caused the problem in the first place so it doesn't happen again.

That's what this book is all about.

IF IT DOESN'T PAN OUT tells you WHY it didn't pan out, and HOW to do it correctly the next time.

The most challenging cooking disasters are those that can be salvaged with imagination. My Aunt Mabel had a wonderfully casual approach to cooking. She seldom worried about how a recipe came out. "If your tomato aspic doesn't gel," she would explain, "you can always serve it as a drink!" But in spite of her creative approach to cooking, even she had occasional failures she could not correct, like the apple pie she once laced with cayenne instead of cinnamon.

There is an element of serendipity to some food disasters from which all of us have benefited. Take the legend (utterly unprovable) of the ancient herdsman who stored his lunch in a cave to keep it cool and then forgot where he had left it. When he came upon it several days later, the cheese looked terrible and smelled even worse. Being desperately hungry, he took a small bite and, to his astonishment, discovered the cheese tasted delicious. This probably was blue cheese, first encountered by chance.

A famous essay by Charles Lamb provides another example. In his fanciful account, a villager removed a pig from the hot ashes of a burned building. In the process, he burned his finger and put it in his mouth to relieve the pain. For the first time, man experienced the delicious taste of roast pig.

Elaborate French sauces were originally created to mask the unpalatable "off" flavor meat tended to develop in the days before refrigeration. Today we still have those magnificent sauces, and we enjoy them even more, because they are used to enhance good food and not to disguise the almost inedible.

The more you cook, the more likely you are to learn how to avoid disasters—and the more apt you are to have new mishaps.

Unless you are one of those rare creatures who always know instinctively how to cook without using measuring cups and spoons or kitchen thermometers and clocks, the best guarantee of success is to follow a reliable, well-written recipe. Take the time to read it all the way through before you start to cook. Avoid cute recipes that tell you to add a "glob of butter," or recipes that call for a "small can" of tomato sauce (how large is small?), or that tell you to add liquid until the batter "looks right." If you read a recipe and find yourself shaking your head, wondering exactly what to do or what to use, throw the recipe (or the book) away.

Are you bothered by the idea of throwing a cookbook out? You shouldn't be. Most cookbooks are not collectors' items. They are tools, just like any other kitchen equipment, and if they don't work, get rid of them.

After you have read the recipe, if you feel reasonably certain it will work, follow it precisely—at least the first time around. When I want to make changes in a recipe, I experiment the second time. And I make careful notes of the changes I've made (and whether they worked!) right on the recipe, because it's important not to trust your memory. Once again, you shouldn't hesitate to write in your cookbooks. Your pencil can be a mighty valuable cooking tool.

Reading a recipe carefully and completely before you begin will eliminate many problems before they arise—like discovering you don't have all the necessary ingredients or the correct-size pan. If a recipe calls for one kind of flour or sugar, you cannot simply substitute another type without risking a change in taste or texture. If a recipe directs you to pour a batter into an 8-inch square pan, you usually cannot use an oblong pan instead without running into serious trouble.

Of course, it is possible to substitute one ingredient for another, one pan for another, to make shortcuts, and to double and triple recipes. But to make these changes successfully, you have to understand the basic principles and avoid the many pitfalls. Each entry in this book was written to help you do just that.

With careful reading of the recipe, you'll know whether you have enough time to prepare the dish properly (some things just can't be rushed) and whether the recipe will yield the number of servings you need. And you'll know if the weather is right! Some recipes, especially those calling for cooked sugar mixtures, just can't be made successfully on rainy days.

Dinner parties provide unique opportunities for disaster. Resist the urge to try a new recipe, especially a complicated and fancy one, when you are expecting company. The experience you gain the first time you prepare a new dish is your insurance against a calamity.

Dinner parties must be well organized if they are to run smoothly. Make a detailed menu and post it in a prominent place so you can refer to it as you begin to serve. It can be pretty distressing, the next day, to discover you forgot to serve a dish you spent hours preparing. When I am getting ready for a party, I put notes all over the kitchen in appropriate places. My oven is likely to wear a reminder that says, "Turn me on at 6:30—400° F." My refrigerator may be decorated with a notation: "Remove cheese at 5:30." This practice is a help to me when I am busy and likely to forget. It is also useful to anyone who may be helping me in the kitchen.

The more you understand the potentials for disaster in the kitchen, the better you will be equipped to avoid them. If you familiarize yourself with the information in this book, you will be able to prevent many disasters and you will gain considerable confidence in yourself as a cook. Add a generous helping of imagination, and you will find your own new and innovative ways to convert disasters into triumphs!

BISCUITS, MUFFINS, AND QUICK BREADS

One of my grandmothers reached the age of forty without ever having learned how to boil water. When necessity placed her in charge of the family cooking, she began by teaching herself to make old-fashioned baking powder biscuits. She used them to dress up almost every meal she served during the first tentative months of her cooking, and thereby managed to convince guests that she was an experienced cook who happened to be serving an unusually simple meal because she was too busy to spend much time in the kitchen. Even when she became a more accomplished cook, her biscuits remained a family favorite.

If you are new to baking, the place to begin is with biscuits, muffins, or quick breads. They are easy to make and, with just a few do's and don'ts securely established in your mind, you should not have any trouble.

Mix dry ingredients thoroughly so they will be evenly distributed throughout the batter.

Don't substitute oil for shortening because liquid cannot be "cut into" dry ingredients properly and a liquid shortening will make your batter gummy.

Batter for quick breads and muffins is not supposed to be thoroughly moistened like cake batter. In fact, if you overmix after you add the liquid, the muffins will be tough and compact and more like cake than bread. Muffins and quick breads are supposed to have little air holes and tunnels.

Spoon batter into muffin tins no more than two-thirds full. If you put too much batter in a muffin tin, the batter will overflow during baking and tops of the muffins will be flat instead of rounded and peaked.

Bake just until lightly browned. Overbaking makes muffins dry and tough.

Remove muffins and quick breads from baking pan as soon as you take them out of the oven. If you allow them to cool in the pan, they will get soggy.

Quick breads are supposed to have a crack down the center. Appearance of a crack is not a cooking mistake; it spells success.

Resist the temptation to slice quick bread before it has cooled. The flavor and moisture in the bread improves with cooling.

Biscuits require less kneading than bread. If you knead too much, the biscuits will not be light and flaky.

When you use a biscuit cutter, cut straight down through the dough. If you twist or turn the cutter, it will give the biscuit a rough edge and a lopsided look.

If you would like to convert a cake recipe into cupcakes, it may help you to know a recipe that fills an 8-inch round pan makes enough batter for about 12 cupcakes, and a recipe for a 9-inch round pan or an 8-inch square pan makes enough batter for about 15 cupcakes.

When you use a cake recipe to make cupcakes, cut the baking time in half.

BREADING

For a great many years I avoided any recipe that called for the breading of food for the simple reason that my breading always fell off. I was firmly convinced that one important ingredient was missing from all the recipes—glue. When I finally succeeded in making breading stick, I was so delighted, my poor family was subjected to endless meals of breaded food so I could practice my new skill.

The best way to bread food successfully is to begin by lining up three dishes (pie plates are ideal). Put seasoned flour in the first dish. Place beaten egg in the second dish and beat in a few drops of cooking oil. If your recipe recommends adding water to the egg, replace the water with oil. If your recipe does not suggest adding anything to the egg, add oil anyway. Put seasoned crumbs in the third dish. I find that fine crumbs adhere best, so I usually use cracker meal.

Pat the food dry with paper towels and place the first piece of food in the flour dish. Use your hands to pat the flour on so the food has a thin, even coating. Then put the flour-coated food in the egg. Make sure the entire piece of food is covered with egg, spooning the egg over it, if necessary. Lift the food with a pair of tongs and hold it over the egg dish until all the excess egg has dripped off. Then put the food in the crumb dish, and using a spoon again, cover the food completely. Finally, use your fingers to pat the crumbs firmly in place. Put the breaded food on a rack covered with waxed paper. When all the food has been breaded and placed on the waxed paper, place the rack in the refrigerator for at least half an hour.

When you are ready to cook, use either clarified butter, a combination of butter or margarine and oil, or shortening. My preference is a combination of butter and oil. Don't use butter or margarine alone because they brown too quickly. Whatever you use, be sure it is hot before you start to cook. Sauté the food over fairly high heat, using tongs to turn the food. If you use a fork, you run the risk of breaking the crumb coating. Don't crowd the pan. Sauté only a few pieces of food at a time. When the food is nicely browned all over, place it on a cookie sheet lined with paper towels and keep it warm in the oven while you cook the remaining food.

Don't try to reheat breaded food in a microwave oven. Microwave cooking is moist cooking and it will turn your carefully made crisp breading into a soggy coating.

If, in spite of all your care and precautions, the breading does not adhere properly, make a quick gravy or sauce to serve over the food and hide the evidence of your difficulty.

BREADS

More than a few people view bread making as an acceptable way to express aggression. For them, kneading has a tension-relieving effect. But whether you make bread as a means of venting emotions or simply because you enjoy eating freshly made bread, you should understand the principles of bread making if you are to be successful.

The most important ingredient in bread is the yeast. It acts as a leavening agent; that is, it causes the dough to rise and makes the bread light. It also helps provide the delicious flavor and wonderful aroma of fresh bread. If you have any doubt whatsoever about whether or not the yeast is active, you must "proof" it before you add any other ingredients. If you use yeast that is no longer alive, the dough will just sit there and you will end up with unleavened bread. Yeast is proofed by dissolving it in warm water and adding one-half teaspoon of sugar. If the yeast is alive it will begin to foam and bubble in about ten minutes. That means you can use it. If it is not alive, throw it away.

The temperature of the water in which yeast is dissolved is critical. If you have prepared an unusually large number of baths for babies, and you are absolutely certain you can gauge the temperature of water on your wrist, you may not need a thermometer. But, since the water must be between 105° F. and 115° F. to dissolve granular yeast, and 95° F. to dissolve compressed yeast, you may be in trouble if you don't use a thermometer. If you guess wrong and the water is too hot, it will kill the yeast and the bread will never rise. If the water is too cold, the bread will rise too slowly.

The dissolved yeast must interact with sugar in order to make the gas that is required to cause the dough to rise. Salt is added to act as a control on the rising process and to bring out the flavor of the bread. Fat is added to the dough to keep the dough elastic and the bread tender and soft. Liquid is necessary to turn the flour into dough. And last, but hardly least, wheat flour provides a protein called gluten that temporarily holds in the gas and provides elasticity and structure to the bread. To these ingredients, a wide range of other kinds of flour and foods can be added to provide different flavors and textures.

Liquids used in bread making should be warm; other ingredients should be room temperature. Cold ingredients slow the rising process. Amounts of flour called for in most recipes are approximate because flours are not standardized throughout the country. Experience will teach you exactly how much flour to use. The total amount of flour used should provide a stiff dough that comes away from the sides of the bowl.

The essence of bread making is proper kneading. You may find it less tiring to work at a kitchen table than at a kitchen counter because the lower height reduces the strain on shoulder muscles while you are kneading.

Form the dough into a ball and place it on a lightly floured surface. Flour your hands and push down on the dough with the heels of your hands, letting your fingers curve over the dough. Give the dough a quarter turn, fold it over, and push down again. Repeat this process, turning and pushing, for about eight to ten minutes. The dough should feel smooth and elastic. If it doesn't, continue to knead two or three minutes longer.

Place the dough in a large well-greased bowl. Turn the dough in the bowl to coat the entire surface with grease. This will prevent the dough from drying out and forming a crust on the surface. Cover with a clean dish towel and set the bowl in a warm, draft-free place. (The center shelf of a cold oven is usually a good choice.) It will take from one hour to an hour and a half for the dough to double in bulk. Press your finger about one inch into the dough. If the indentation remains, the dough is ready.

Bring your aggressive nature to the fore, make a fist, and punch down in the center of the dough. (You will be able to hear the air whoosh out.) Punch the edges down lightly and turn the dough out onto a lightly floured surface. Let it rest ten to fifteen minutes to recover from the beating you have given it.

Divide the dough and form loaves that will fill loaf pans no more than two-thirds full. Gently pinch ends and tuck pinched ends under. Place in well-greased pans, cover with dish towels, and return to a warm, draft-free place. The dough will rise again, usually more quickly than it rose the first time. Allow the dough to rise slightly above the tops of the pans, forming a nicely rounded loaf.

If bread has been rising in the oven, remove it. Preheat oven, brush top of bread with egg wash (a beaten egg mixed with one tablespoon water), and bake according to directions in recipe.

When bread is baked, remove it from the pan immediately and cool it on a rack. If you tap the bottom of the bread with your knuckles and it sounds hollow, the bread is a success!

A few bread baking cautions:

There is no way you can hurry the rising process. If, for example, you place the dough on top of a radiator to speed things up, the dough will rise only once and will lose its elasticity.

If the dough has risen too high in the pan, don't put it in the oven that way; it probably will collapse while it is baking. Instead, punch the dough down a second time, reshape it, and let it rise a third time.

Kneading activates the gluten in the flour. If you don't knead long enough the bread will not rise as high as it should. If you knead too long you may get large holes in your bread, which, when you think about it, is not all that terrible. In other words, overkneading is certainly preferable to underkneading.

If your bread takes on a really strange shape, the chances are good you used a pan too small for the amount of dough.

Even the first time you make bread, your results should be satisfactory, if you follow a good recipe carefully, remember the rules of bread making, use well-made bread pans, and remember to preheat your oven. You may decide it takes practice to become a really accomplished bread baker, but it can be done, and it certainly is worth the effort.

QUICK SOLUTIONS

Texture of bread is fine, but shape is distressing

- Slice bread in the kitchen.
- Cut into cubes, sauté or toast in the oven, and use as croutons.
- Toast and use under food such as Welsh rabbit, chipped beef, or poached eggs.

Bread is soggy

- Slice and toast.
- Hollow out center of loaf and fill with food such as crab Newburg or chicken à la king.
- Cut into cubes and make bread pudding.
- Use for stuffing.
- Slice and use for French toast.
- Use in any recipe that calls for bread soaked in milk or water.
- Use in recipes that call for layers of sliced bread, such as cheese strata.

Bread is too dry

- Make bread crumbs.
- Use for croutons.
- Cut into cubes, soften with broth, and use for stuffing.
- Use in any recipe that calls for soaked bread or layers of bread.
- Heat briefly in microwave oven to soften.

CHECKLIST FOR NEXT TIME

Problem	Probable Cause
Bread is soggy or sags in middle	– Did you add too much liquid to the dough? – Did you stop kneading too soon?
Bread flat and doughy	– Did you let dough rise too long the second time?
Bread uneven	– Did you forget to bake bread in center of oven?

Problem	Probable Cause
Bread did not rise enough	– Were ingredients too hot?
	– Were ingredients too cold?
	– Did you underknead?
	– Was oven temperature too low?
Bottom and sides of bread soft and soggy	– Did you forget to remove bread from pan as soon as you took it out of the oven?
	– Did you forget to cool bread on rack?
	– Did you cool bread in draft?
	– Did you wrap it for storage while still warm?
Bread mushrooms in center	– Was pan too small?
	– Was oven too hot?
Large holes in bread	– Did you overknead?
	– Did you let dough rise too long the second time?
Small hard lumps of dough in bread	– Was dough inadequately mixed before kneading?
Large circles in center of rolled bread	– Was bread rolled too tightly?
	– Were ends of bread pinched too tightly?

CAKES

There are many cooks who feel the best guarantee of successful cake making is to use a cake mix. But while there are many excellent cake mixes on the market, even they can prove disastrous if they are not mixed and baked properly. And although it certainly is true that cake mixes can save time, it is also true that a cake made from them costs more than the same cake made from scratch. Whichever way you decide to make a cake, your best guarantee of success is understanding the principles of cake making.

Most baking recipes are exact chemical formulas that cannot be changed without risking failure. Nowhere in cooking are exact measurements, correct pan sizes, accurate oven temperatures, and specified ingredients more important. Any changes you want to make in a properly tested recipe must be carefully thought through. Obviously you can substitute orange juice for lemon juice, or pecans for walnuts, if you want to make a change in flavor. But, for example, you cannot simply substitute one cup of all-purpose flour for one cup of cake flour. In order for the chemistry to work correctly, you must use one cup less two tablespoons of all-purpose flour for every cup of cake flour in the recipe.

For the best chance of success, assemble all the ingredients and the correct-size pans before you begin.

All ingredients should be at room temperature (about 75° F.) before they are combined. This means refrigerated food such as butter, margarine, eggs, or milk should be removed from the refrigerator at least one hour before you are ready to start baking. It also means that melted ingredients, such as butter or chocolate, should be melted long enough in advance to have cooled to room temperature (but not solidified) before you add them to the batter. But remember: if eggs are to be separated, separate them while they are still cold and allow them to come to room temperature. (Place yolks in covered container.)

Use well-made pans and prepare them as the recipe directs. Then set them aside.

Measure the ingredients carefully, using dry or liquid measuring cups as appropriate.

Preheat the oven ten to fifteen minutes before you are ready to use it and check the temperature with an oven thermometer to be certain you will be baking at the specified temperature.

Follow instructions exactly regarding the way in which ingredients are mixed and the order in which they are combined. Be careful not to overmix, because overmixing will make the batter heavy and, in turn, the cake heavy.

The correct pan size is always included in a baking recipe. If you decide to use a different pan size you probably will get into trouble. The pan size called for is related to the amount of batter in the recipe and to the kind of cake you are making. If your recipe calls for two round 9-inch pans, and you decide to use two round 8-inch pans instead, obviously you will have problems because you will have too much batter. When you make a substitution, the capacity of the pans called for and the pans you substitute must be the same. But even when the capacity is the same, a cake that is supposed to be baked in a flat pan should never be baked in a tube or loaf pan. However, the reverse will work, and you can substitute a flat pan of comparable capacity in a recipe that calls for a high pan. When you change the size of the pan, watch your cake carefully. It probably will be necessary to adjust baking time. And, if you use a glass baking dish instead of a metal one, you must reduce the oven temperature by 25°F.

The following chart should prove helpful in an emergency when you must make a substitution for the pan size called for:

4 cup (1-quart) capacity:	9-inch pie plate
	8-inch round cake pan
	7 x 3 x 2-inch loaf pan
4 ½ cup capacity:	8 x 2¼-inch ring mold

6 cup (1½-quart) capacity:	9-inch round cake pan
	10-inch pie plate
	8 x 3 x 2-inch loaf pan
	7-inch tube pan
8 cup (2-quart) capacity:	8-inch square baking dish
	11 x 7 x 1½-inch baking dish
	9 x 5 x 3-inch loaf pan
	9½-inch brioche pan
9 cup capacity:	9-inch tube or bundt pan
10 cup (2½-quart) capacity:	9-inch square pan
	15 x 10 x 1-inch jelly roll pan
12 cup (3-quart) capacity:	13 x 8 x 2-inch baking dish
	9 x 3½-inch angel cake pan
	10-inch tube or bundt pan
	8 x 3-inch springform pan
15 cup capacity:	13 x 9 x 2-inch baking dish
16 cup (4-quart) capacity:	10 x 4-inch tube mold
	10-inch kugelhof pan
	9 x 3-inch springform pan
18 cup (4½-quart) capacity:	10 x 4-inch angel cake pan

Pour the batter into the prepared pans, making certain the batter is evenly distributed. Tap the pans gently on a flat surface to remove excess air bubbles.

Check once more to be certain the oven is the correct temperature. Place the pans on the middle shelf in the center of the oven. Don't let the pans touch each other or the sides of the oven because air must be able to circulate freely around the pans.

Set a timer for the minimum amount of time given in the recipe and check the cake at that time to see if it is done. If necessary, return the cake to the oven for a few minutes longer. Then check again.

Remove the pans from the oven and follow recipe directions for cooling. Most cakes are cooled in the pan long enough for the cake to pull away from the sides of the pan. Once this has happened it should be a simple matter to remove the cakes from the pans and finish cooling them on racks. Angel food cakes and chiffon cakes are handled differently and need more care. Follow the instructions in your recipe exactly for best results.

Allow the cakes to cool completely before frosting.

If you follow all of the rules carefully and you use a reliable recipe, you should not have any problems.

If a cake doesn't turn out as expected and the problem is primarily visual, there are several things you can do.

Icings, frostings, and whipped cream can be used to cover a multitude of sins. If the top of your cake has a bump or too heavy a crust, cut the top off, turn the cake upside down, and cover it with a glaze or icing. You really don't have to take a course in cake decorating in order to cover a cake smoothly and carefully. And if you feel it doesn't look even enough, you can always add chopped nuts or bits of chocolate.

Another good solution is to cut an awkward looking cake in the kitchen. If you cut it into squares, it will probably look as though you had intended to serve it this way in the first place. Place each square on a serving dish and cover with Hot Fudge Sauce Supreme, Blueberry-Brandy Sauce, or flavored whipped cream.

Hot Fudge Sauce Supreme   MAKES ABOUT 2 CUPS

¾ cup half and half
1¾ cups sugar
3 tablespoons light corn syrup
3 squares (3 ounces) unsweetened chocolate
3 tablespoons butter
1 teaspoon vanilla
½ teaspoon salt

Place cream, sugar, and syrup in medium-size saucepan and cook over moderate heat, stirring constantly, until mixture comes to a boil. Lower heat and simmer until sugar is dissolved, stirring constantly. Remove pan from heat, add chocolate and stir until melted. Add butter, vanilla, and salt and stir until butter is melted. Serve warm, spooned over your favorite cake, ice cream, soufflé, or frozen dessert.

Blueberry-Brandy Sauce   MAKES ABOUT 2½ CUPS

2 cups fresh blueberries or 1 package (12 ounces)
frozen blueberries, slightly thawed

1 **cup sugar**
1½ **tablespoons cornstarch**
⅛ **teaspoon salt**
2 **tablespoons brandy**
2 **teaspoons lemon juice**

Bring 1 cup water to a boil in medium-size saucepan. Add blueberries and simmer. Combine sugar, cornstarch, and salt; mix well and add to saucepan. Cook over moderate heat, stirring constantly, until thickened. Remove from heat, stir in brandy and lemon juice. Cool slightly and spoon over cake, frozen dessert, soufflé, or pancakes.

NICE TO KNOW: If you have a 16-ounce package of frozen blueberries, measure out the amount needed and reserve the remainder for another time. If you have fresh blueberries that are not quite as fresh as they ought to be, you can still use them to make this delicious sauce. For variety, substitute raspberries or strawberries, or use a combination of berries.

When a cake is too dry, cut it into squares, pour rum or brandy over the cake, cover, and let it stand about one hour to absorb the liquor. Then place the squares on individual serving dishes and top with whipped cream.

When a solid cake like pound cake is too dry or has become stale, you can cut it into cubes and dip it in melted chocolate at the table, fondue fashion. Or you might put pieces of it in the bottom of a dish and spoon fruit over it for a special fruit dessert, use it to make a cake-based bread pudding, or even broil it lightly and serve it with warm fruit.

When an angel food cake falls, it is heavy, gummy, and not very appetizing. Don't throw it away. Make Chocolate Angel Delight instead.

Chocolate Angel Delight   SERVES 8 TO 10

½ **fallen angel food cake**
1 **package (6 ounces) semisweet chocolate morsels**
4 **eggs, beaten**
1 **cup heavy cream, whipped**
1 **teaspoon almond extract**
1 **cup chopped almonds (or whatever nuts you have on hand), divided**

Cut cake into bite-size pieces or small cubes and place in bottom of 13 x 9 x 2-inch baking dish. Melt chocolate in top of double boiler; remove from heat and let cool slightly. Slowly add eggs to chocolate, beating until well combined. Pour chocolate mixture into large bowl and fold in whipped cream. Add almond extract and ½ cup chopped almonds, and stir. Slowly drizzle chocolate mixture over cake. Sprinkle with remaining ½ cup nuts and refrigerate several hours until firm. Cut into square portions and serve.

NOTE: If you want to use all of the fallen cake, double the chocolate recipe and divide cake into 2 pans. (You can freeze 1.) Or, double the chocolate recipe and make dessert in layers.

If your cake is a hopeless disaster or if you have stale cake on hand, put it in a blender or food processor, a few pieces at a time, and turn it into cake crumbs. Use the crumbs to make Banana-Coconut Crumb Delight.

Banana-Coconut Crumb Delight　　SERVES 6

1 medium-size ripe banana	⅓ cup chopped pecans
½ teaspoon lemon juice	¾ cup heavy cream
2½ cups cake crumbs	2 egg whites
⅓ cup dark seedless raisins	¼ cup sugar
⅓ cup shredded coconut	

Place banana in large mixing bowl, mash with fork, and sprinkle with lemon juice. Add crumbs, raisins, coconut, and pecans, and stir to combine. Whip cream until stiff and fold into crumb mixture. Wash beaters, beat egg whites in clean bowl until slightly thickened, sprinkle with sugar, and continue beating until stiff. Fold beaten egg whites into whipped-cream mixture until thoroughly combined. Spoon mixture into 1-quart dish, cover, and freeze until firm. Remove from freezer 20 minutes before serving. Or, to make special treats for the children, line muffin pan with cupcake liners and spoon mixture into liners. Cover and freeze until firm.

QUICK SOLUTIONS

Cake looks terrible

- Cover cake with icing, whipped cream, fruit, a dusting of confectioners sugar, or ice cream.
- Cut cake into serving portions in the kitchen, and top each slice with one of the above.
- Slice off uneven top of cake and turn upside down before icing.
- Slice cake into several thin layers, frost between layers, and cover with frosting to make a multilayer cake.
- Cut into squares and top each square with fruit.

Cake is too dry

- Soak with rum, brandy, or a good syrup.
- Cut cake into cubes and serve with chocolate fondue.
- Make an English trifle or *zuppa inglese*.

Cake is too soggy

- Slice and toast.

Hopeless failure

- Turn into cake crumbs and use in baked fruit desserts.

CHECKLIST FOR NEXT TIME

Problem	Probable Cause
Coarse grainy texture	– Did you beat batter too short a time? – Was the oven temperature too high?
Heavy texture	– Did you overbeat batter? – Did you fail to measure ingredients accurately? – Was the oven temperature too low?
Dry texture	– Did you bake the cake too long? – Was the oven temperature too high?

Problem	Probable Cause
Cake falls	– Did you bake the cake too short a time? – Was the pan too small? – Was the oven temperature either too high or too low? – Did you open the oven door too soon? – Was the cake jarred?
Wrinkled top or poor volume	– Did you overmix the batter? – Did you add too much liquid? – Was the pan too large? – Was the cake baked too short a time? – Was the oven temperature too low?
Cracks or humps on top	– Was pan too small? – Was oven temperature too high?
Sticky top	– Did you add too much liquid? – Was the cake baked too short a time? – Did you bake on a day when the humidity was very high? – Was the oven temperature too low?
Cake stuck in pan	– Did you forget to grease and flour cake pans carefully? – Was the cake left to cool in pan too long?

CHICKEN

When chickens carry brand names and the president of a chicken-producing company becomes a television celebrity, chickens have arrived. And chicken deserves its popularity. In spite of inflation, it still is one of the most economical foods available and one of the most versatile.

Chicken probably can be cooked in more different ways than almost any other food. And there aren't really many things you can do to a chicken that are likely to end in a serious disaster. Southern fried chicken probably has the greatest potential for failure. But if you learn how to bread food properly (see chapter on Breading), even that is not impossibly difficult. Good flavoring and correct timing are the most important things about cooking chicken properly. Undercooking will tend to leave the chicken tough; overcooking will dry out the meat. Proper cooking time depends not only on the age and size of the chicken, but on the cooking method. For example, a boneless chicken breast takes only fifteen to twenty minutes of gentle poaching to be fully cooked. That same breast, still firmly attached to a roaster, will take at least two hours of roasting before it is ready to eat.

All chicken benefits from cooking by low heat, and in the long run, undercooking chicken is far better than overcooking it. One reason some cooks tend to overcook chicken is to eliminate the pink color sometimes found on the bone. However, this pink color does not necessarily indicate undercooking, and its presence will not affect the flavor of the chicken.

Chickens have considerably more natural fat these days than they used to have. This fact has brought about some changes in cooking methods. When I first started cooking, it was impossible to broil chicken properly without brushing it periodically with butter or margarine. This is no longer necessary, because as the chicken broils, the fat melts and it can be used for basting. Additional fat is not necessary. In fact there often is more natural fat than needed. The presence of this extra natural fat has also reduced the amount of additional fat necessary to baste roasting poultry, although some butter or margarine should be used at the very beginning of roasting in order to keep the skin from drying out.

Taste is not the only sense that helps us determine whether or not a food is appetizing. Eye appeal is important, too. Pale poultry skin can be very distasteful looking. A liberal coating of paprika on the skin will produce a beautiful golden color. If you use imported paprika that has flavor, as opposed to domestic paprika that does not, you may find it will eliminate the need for ground pepper. If you use both, the skin may be too spicy.

There are no rules more important for roasting poultry than those provided by the U.S. government regarding safe methods for cooking stuffing. The only safe procedure is to stuff the cavity of a bird immediately before you put it in a hot oven. Since the cavity of an uncooked bird has a very high bacteria count, it is possible for the stuffing to become contaminated if it is not cooked immediately. Stuffing provides an extremely hospitable spot for the rapid growth of bacteria. Refrigeration does not solve the problem. So it is important to remember that it is not safe to try to get the jump on preparations for a Christmas or Thanksgiving dinner by stuffing your turkey the night before you plan to cook it.

You can determine whether or not poultry is fully cooked by making sure the juices are a clear yellow and the drumstick moves easily. But you cannot determine if the stuffing is fully cooked, and safe to eat, unless you use a meat thermometer. The center of the stuffing must reach a temperature of 165° F. Leftover stuffing should not be left inside a cooked bird either. Remove stuffing, cover it, store in the refrigerator, and reheat separately.

Learning how to split, quarter, or cut a chicken into eighths is not difficult. Whenever I buy chicken, I check prices to see if the butcher has charged extra to cut it. If he has, I buy a whole chicken and cut it myself. You can split a chicken down the center of the breast bone in less than a minute with poultry shears or a sharp boning knife. It's an easy chore that certainly is not worth paying someone else to do for you. If you want to quarter the chicken, divide the split chicken down the back, then divide each half at the point where the thigh meets the body of the chicken. And if you want to divide the chicken even further, separate the thighs from the drumsticks and the wings from the breasts.

I often cut off the wing tips and backbone and store them in my freezer along with the necks and giblets. When I have a reasonably good supply, I use them to make chicken soup or stock. Sometimes, instead, I cook the giblets separately, chop them, and store them in the freezer, ready to be added to stuffing or gravy. You can also freeze the chicken livers separately and keep them until you have enough to make sautéed chicken livers or chopped chicken liver. Caution: Livers cannot be stored in the freezer indefinitely.

The flavor of many dishes is enhanced by chicken fat. I view the extra fat on a chicken as a kind of special bonus. When I clean a chicken I pull off all the excess fat, drop it in a pot of boiling water, and cook it until the fat has been rendered and most of the water has boiled away. Then I strain it, place it in a covered jar, and store it in the freezer. Any water that has not cooked away settles on the bottom of the jar. The fat that rises to the top of the jar is pure chicken fat. (Most of the rendered chicken fat sold in supermarkets has had preservatives added.) Use the chicken fat in place of butter, margarine, or oil to sauté any food that you want to flavor with chicken.

Both duck and goose have much more fat than chicken or turkey and require some special attention. They must be well pricked so the fat can drain out, otherwise the finished dish will be fatty and the skin will not be crisp.

In the event you overcook poultry and find it too dry to eat, the best suggestion is to remove all the meat from the bones, discard the skin, and cut the meat into small pieces. Cooked poultry cubes or slivers can be used in soup or can be turned into a lovely salad, provided enough salad dressing is used to add moisture to the dry meat. Adding overcooked poultry to a casserole is not likely to be very successful if additional cooking will be required, because unless there is a substantial amount of liquid in the casserole, the meat will dry out even further. Overcooked poultry can, however, be mixed with a sauce and turned into a dish like chicken à la king, because all that is necessary is gentle heating, rather than additional cooking.

One of the nicest things about cooking poultry is that whether you prepare it by the simplest method possible or turn it into an elaborate company dish, it can always be used as the focal point of a satisfying meal.

QUICK SOLUTIONS

Chicken is overcooked or tough

- Remove skin and bones:
    cut into cubes and serve as salad or serve hot with sauce;
    finely chop in meat grinder or food processor, bind with thickener, season, and use in an omelet, in crepes, or as pasta stuffing.

Chicken bone is pink near joints

- If meat is tender, serve as is.
- If meat is not tender, continue cooking.

Chicken is done, but skin is still pale

- Rub skin with paprika or baste with browned drippings and cook just a little longer.
- Run briefly under broiler.

Skin is browned, but meat is not done

- Cover with foil and continue cooking.

CHECKLIST FOR NEXT TIME

Problem	Probable Cause
Chicken tough	– Did you cook it too short a time?
Chicken still tough after additional cooking	– Did you buy a chicken too old for your cooking method?

Problem	Probable Cause
Chicken dry	– Did you cook it too long?
	– Did you forget to baste during roasting?
	– Did you forget to cover, if preparing a casserole?
Skin browned before meat was done	– Was oven temperature too high?
Breading falls off fried chicken	– See chapter on Breading.

CHOCOLATE

Undoubtedly chocolate is the most popular cake and icing flavoring. A friend of mine calls every year without fail to find out if I am planning to serve at least one chocolate dessert on New Year's Eve, and then obligingly follows her inquiry with an offer to make one if I am not. No matter how many desserts I serve, it is always the chocolate treats that disappear first. There is a big difference in flavor between really good chocolate and the ordinary, everyday chocolate available in the supermarket. So, when I expect company, I usually splurge and buy the better chocolate. All chocolate is expensive these days, and the better the chocolate, the more expensive it is. Therefore, if you are going to invest a small fortune in chocolate, it is particularly important to know how to handle it.

Weather can be a major factor if you want chocolate to set properly. Restrict your cooking to a day when the humidity is low and the temperature can be controlled and set at about 65° F. Be sure your work area is draft-free. Temperature, humidity, and drafts are all contributing factors when chocolate does not set properly.

Caution: Use controlled low heat to melt chocolate. It burns easily, and if it does, there is nothing you can do except throw it away. The best way to melt chocolate by itself is in the top of a double boiler sitting over (not in) simmering water. Before the chocolate is completely melted, remove the top half of the double boiler and let the melting finish, off the heat. Another caution: It is very important that moisture not get into the melting chocolate—not even a single drop. This means, above all else, that the double boiler cannot be covered, because moisture will collect under the cover and drop into the chocolate. If this happens, the chocolate "stiffens" and is virtually impossible to spread. But don't despair. You don't have to throw out the chocolate. You can remedy the situation by adding one teaspoon of vegetable shortening for every ounce of chocolate being melted. Do not add butter to stiffened chocolate, because butter contains water and will only worsen the situation.

Just about every microwave-oven cookbook recommends melting wrapped chocolate in the microwave oven. I find this an unsatisfactory way to melt chocolate for two reasons. It is of no benefit to chocolate to melt it quickly, and I have never been able to scrape the melted chocolate off the paper without making a horrendous mess. In the end, microwaving is not really a timesaver and it is a waste of chocolate.

Occasionally chocolate that has been stored in a warm place develops a gray film, referred to as a "bloom." This does not mean the chocolate has gone bad. It still can be melted and used effectively in a recipe.

Most recipes that call for cocoa mean unsweetened cocoa. I prefer the Dutch-process cocoa, which doesn't necessarily come from Holland any more, but which does have a marvelous flavor. When a recipe calls for chocolate and you don't have any on hand, you can substitute three tablespoons of cocoa and two teaspoons of shortening for every ounce of unsweetened chocolate called for. If you need either sweet or semisweet chocolate, just add a little granulated sugar to taste.

Several years ago, I persuaded an aunt to give me a recipe for a chocolate dessert she often served. Since she couldn't tell me, I don't know where it came from. But I do know this rather odd recipe has been a family favorite for many years, in spite of the unfortunate name we have given it. It isn't a cake in the traditional sense, but it is absolutely fail-proof and ideal to make in an emergency.

Aunt Bea's Foolproof Chocolate Mess   SERVES 10

2 cups granulated sugar, divided
2 cups all-purpose flour
4 teaspoons baking powder
¼ teaspoon salt

   2 ounces (2 squares) unsweetened chocolate
   ¼ cup butter
   1 cup milk
   ½ cup finely chopped nuts
   1 teaspoon vanilla
   ⅔ cup firmly packed dark brown sugar
   6 tablespoons unsweetened cocoa (Dutch-process cocoa preferred)
      Whipped cream

Preheat oven to 350° F. Sift 1⅓ cups granulated sugar, flour, baking powder, and salt together, and set aside. Melt chocolate and butter in small saucepan; add to flour mixture and stir. Add milk, nuts, and vanilla and stir. Spread batter in deep 2½-quart buttered dish. Scatter brown sugar, remaining ⅔ cup granulated sugar, and cocoa on top of batter. Pour 2 cups water over entire mess. Do not stir! Bake in preheated oven 1 hour. When done, there will be a crust on top and chocolate will be runny inside. Serve hot with whipped cream.

COFFEE
AND
TEA

A fierce-looking lion with a message sits above my coffeepot: "I'm not worth a damn until I've had my morning coffee." He was a gift from one of my daughters, who thought the lion and I had something in common. I don't think I am a real coffee addict because I can take it or leave it during the day. But I do like a good cup of strong coffee first thing in the morning and as the final touch to a good dinner. What little English ancestry I have must have been lost entirely, because on those rare occasions when I express a preference for hot tea, my family is likely to call a doctor before they make the tea.

Obviously, the question of whether to drink coffee or tea (or anything else) is a matter of personal preference. And undoubtedly many people are perfectly content with instant coffee or a trusty tea bag. But even if you find quick-drink methods satisfactory on a day-to-day basis, as a good hostess you probably will want to provide the real thing for guests. A poorly made cup of tea or coffee is a disaster for one who cares.

Coffee

Coffee making must begin with a very clean pot because coffee residue makes coffee bitter. Use fresh coffee, correctly ground for the kind of pot you are using. The right proportion of coffee to water depends, to some extent, on the temperamental nature of your coffeepot and, to a large extent, on how strong you want the coffee to be. The average proportion is a standard coffee measure (or two level tablespoons) of coffee for every *six* ounces of fresh cold water. (A coffee cup does not hold eight ounces.) Measure carefully; don't guess. If your coffeepot requires a disposable filter, use a fresh filter every time you make coffee. Serve the coffee very hot, as soon as possible after it has been brewed.

When you serve iced coffee, be careful not to make the mistake of diluting good coffee with ice cubes. If you have time, make ice cubes out of coffee. If you don't have time to do that, make extra-strong coffee that will still be strong enough to drink after ice cubes have been added. And do have cream on hand to add to iced coffee. You may discover that many people who ordinarily drink hot coffee black enjoy adding cream to iced coffee.

Tea

Methods for making hot tea can range from the simplicity of pouring boiling water over a tea bag in a cup, all the way to the charm and elegance of a Japanese tea ceremony. Somewhere between these extremes is an easy but precise method for making fine tea.

Properly brewed tea cannot be made in a metal pot. Select a china or ceramic pot and warm it by filling it with boiling water. (Discard the water before you make the tea.) Place one teaspoon of tea (or one tea bag) in the teapot for every cup of tea you want to make. Then add an additional teaspoonful "for the pot." Bring fresh cold water to a rolling boil and pour in six ounces of boiling water for each cup of tea you are making. Stir well, cover, let the tea steep about five minutes, strain (or remove the tea bags), and serve promptly.

Even non-tea drinkers often view iced tea as a summer treat. You can, if you like, simply make strong tea, pour it over ice cubes, stir in superfine sugar (it will dissolve more quickly than granulated sugar) and lemon juice, and serve the tea topped with a sprig of fresh mint. However, the flavor of iced tea is considerably improved if you add the sugar, lemon juice, lemon rinds, and mint, if available, to the pot of steeping tea. Let it steep at least half an hour, then strain the tea, allow it to come to room temperature, and store it in the refrigerator, ready to drink at any time. If you place a pitcher of hot tea in the refrigerator, the tea will get cloudy. This change in appearance is unattractive, but will not affect the flavor. Cloudiness can be removed by adding a small amount of boiling water to the cloudy tea.

A few months ago my husband and I—in self defense—gave a new automatic coffeepot to favorite relatives whom we love to visit. We had concluded this was the only way we could improve the quality of the coffee they served—and we were right. This particular solution, admittedly somewhat drastic, may not be appropriate in every situation, but it does illustrate how important it is to use the proper equipment if you really want to make a good cup of tea or coffee. And, if someone unexpectedly presents you with a new coffeepot or teapot, perhaps you had better review the methods you have been using to prepare coffee or tea. Once you have learned how to do it properly, it will become second nature.

EGGS

Eggs may be small, but the role they play in cooking certainly is not. Anyone on a low-cholesterol diet knows there are a wide variety of dishes that are forbidden or restricted because eggs are included in the recipe. These neatly packaged marvels have an almost magical quality because they serve so many different cooking functions.

The delicate nature of eggs makes it necessary to handle them with care whether you are cooking a whole egg, using just the yolk, or whipping up egg whites. The one rule that applies to just about every phase of egg cookery is that eggs should be cooked with moderate or low heat.

The exception to this rule is omelette making, when moderate to high heat is appropriate. As a matter of fact, it is because controlled heat is so important that knowledgeable food writers no longer use the descriptions "hard-boiled" and "soft-boiled" eggs. They have substituted "hard-cooked" and "soft-cooked," because even when an egg is still in its shell, it should not be subjected to high heat.

Although the process of preparing soft-cooked or hard-cooked eggs does not seem complicated enough to justify an undue amount of discussion, our foremost cooking experts often devote time to the subject. They know that many people encounter difficulty peeling eggs smoothly, getting the eggs cooked without having them crack, cooking them to the exact degree of doneness desired, or keeping them from developing an unsightly greenish ring around the yolk when they have been hard-cooked.

To prevent an egg from cracking during cooking, pierce the large end with an egg piercer or a straight pin before you cook it. Some experts suggest adding either salt or vinegar to the cooking water. This will not prevent eggs from cracking but it will quite effectively stem the flow of egg white. But piercing the egg really will help to prevent cracking.

How long an egg should be cooked can be a ridiculously complicated question. Just about everyone has had the experience of ordering a five-minute egg in a restaurant and getting an egg that does not remotely resemble either the five-minute egg served in another restaurant or one cooked at home. Many factors go into the timing of an egg. Was the egg placed in water directly from the refrigerator, or was the egg at room temperature? Was the water cold, or was it already simmering when the egg was placed in the pot? What happened to the egg when the five minutes were up? Was the heat turned off and the egg allowed to sit in the warm water—even for a minute? Was the egg removed from the water immediately and plunged into cold water? Or was the egg removed from the cooking water and served immediately? Even the size of the egg can affect the amount of cooking time necessary. Since all these factors affect the way the egg will turn out, my best suggestion is to decide on a method that proves satisfactory for you—starting with either room-temperature or cold eggs, simmering or cold water, with the size eggs you customarily use—and stick to it. Then you will be able to work out the timing that is just right for you. But remember, if you change the procedure for any of the steps, you'll change the results, too.

A greenish ring sometimes develops around the yolk of a hard-cooked egg. It isn't harmful, but it isn't beautiful either. Its presence means the egg was cooked over too-high heat, cooked too long, or had been stored for several days after cooking. If you are careful to cook eggs over moderate heat and use them within a few days, you are not likely to have a greenish ring.

Since I rarely have difficulty peeling hard-cooked eggs, and since I always pierce them before I cook them, I suspect there is a connection between these two facts. Scientifically speaking, the fresher the egg, the harder it will be to peel. If you purchase eggs in a supermarket, the chances are pretty good the eggs were not laid within the previous twenty-four hours. But if the eggs you buy are truly farm fresh, get them several days before you plan to hard-cook them.

Eggs separate best when they are cold. If your recipe calls for egg yolks or egg whites, separate them as soon as you remove them from the refrigerator. One problem cooks sometimes encounter is that of keeping a broken yolk out of a bowl of separated whites when an egg unexpectedly breaks. This problem can be avoided by dividing each egg, as it is cracked, into two small containers and then transferring the separated whites and yolks into larger bowls before cracking the next egg.

The volume of beaten egg whites is increased when the whites are allowed to come to room temperature before they are beaten. So you should separate your cold eggs well ahead of time and set the egg whites to one side to warm up before you beat them. Cream of tartar will help stabilize beaten egg whites. If you beat them in an unlined copper bowl, you don't really need to add cream of tartar. The chemical reaction that takes place in an unlined copper bowl will stabilize them. Caution: Don't beat egg whites in an aluminum bowl because they will darken.

Once egg whites have been beaten, fold them immediately into the food they are to be combined with. The longer egg whites stand, the more volume they lose. In the event they get runny they cannot be rebeaten.

Folding and stirring are not the same thing. If you stir beaten egg whites into a mixture, air will be lost and their volume will be reduced. The best way to fold (and this applies to whipped cream, as well) is to take a small amount of beaten egg white and stir it into the mixture to lighten it. Then spoon the balance of the beaten egg whites on top of the lightened mixture and, using a rubber spatula, make circular "down-over-up-over" motions, turning the bowl with your other hand as you work. Where folding is concerned, I keep coming across recipes that seem to be written backwards. If a recipe tells you to fold a mixture *into* beaten egg whites, ignore the instructions and do it the correct way instead by *folding the egg whites into the mixture.* Your ingredients will retain much greater volume that way.

Handling egg yolks is by far the trickiest aspect of cooking with eggs. Yolks are often used as a thickening agent, and roughly speaking, two egg yolks equal approximately one tablespoon of flour. But you can't just add beaten egg yolks to a hot mixture—unless, of course, you are making egg drop soup. The temperature of the egg yolks must be raised very gradually in order to keep them from turning into scrambled eggs. In order to do this, beat the egg yolks first, then add a very small amount of hot mixture to the beaten yolks, blending vigorously as you add the hot liquid. Keep adding hot liquid slowly until the temperature of the yolks has been raised. Then, and only then, should you pour the egg yolks back into the sauce—slowly—beating as you do it.

If you're thinking of using eggs in a way you have never used them before, take the time to check a reliable cookbook so you will know the correct cooking procedure. A great many years ago, when I was a new bride, unexpected company appeared around dinner time and I decided to turn the only meat I had available into meat loaf instead of hamburgers. I remembered that my grandmother had always served meat loaf with a hard-cooked egg in the center—a nice touch for company. So, after I had shaped the meat loaf, I hollowed out a hole in the center, carefully broke an egg into it, covered the egg with the meat, and put my dinner in the oven to cook. Of course when I cut the cooked meat at the dinner table the egg was still raw, because the heat in the center of the meat had never gotten high enough to cook the egg white or the yolk. It is not the sort of mistake someone is likely to make more than once, and it taught me to check carefully before I try an entirely new procedure, particularly where eggs are concerned.

QUICK SOLUTIONS

Supposedly hard-cooked egg is too soft

• Scramble and cook quickly in a small amount of butter.

Supposedly soft-cooked egg is too hard

• Start over with new eggs.
• Chill hard-cooked eggs for later use. Chop, slice, or quarter and use as egg salad, in a casserole, or as a garnish.
• Make deviled eggs.

Eggs won't peel properly and therefore look dreadful

• Chop or sieve and use as a salad or as a garnish.

CHECKLIST FOR NEXT TIME

Problem	Probable Cause
Shells crack while cooking	– Did you forget to pierce shells before cooking?
Carefully timed eggs are too soft	– Did you forget to increase the time for eggs at refrigerator temperature? – Did you forget to place eggs in simmering, not cold, water?
Carefully timed eggs are too hard	– Did you allow eggs to sit in hot water after they had finished cooking?
Hard-cooked eggs have greenish rings around yolks	– Did you store cooked eggs in refrigerator too long? – Did you cook eggs at too high a temperature?
Hard-cooked eggs won't peel	– Were eggs too fresh? – Did you forget to pierce shells before cooking?
White portion of fried egg is like rubber	– Was heat too high? – Were eggs cooked too long?
Sauces or dishes made with egg yolks curdle	– Did you heat egg yolks too quickly, by adding yolks to a hot mixture, for example, or by adding a hot ingredient to eggs, all at once? – Was the heat too high? – Did you cook sauce or dish too long? – Did you add oil or fat too quickly?
Eggs won't separate properly	– Did you forget to separate eggs while they were still cold?

FISH

There was a time when fish was considered the most economical meal you could serve. Unfortunately, the only people who still think fish is economical are those who catch it themselves. But the cost of fish is not the only thing that has changed. Many varieties of fish that used to be plentiful have become relatively scarce, and types of fish that were not considered marketable at one time are becoming increasingly popular.

Nevertheless, it is not only the cost of fish that often keeps it off the family menu. Many cooks hesitate to buy a fish they are not familiar with because they are not sure how to cook it properly. In fact, there are a surprising number of cooks who genuinely like fish but almost never cook it, because they don't know what to do with it when they get it home. Actually, there are few foods easier to cook than fish.

Fish can be bought whole, filleted, or cut into steaks. A whole fish costs less per pound than fish that has been cut because whole fish is weighed and priced before it is cleaned or dressed, so you pay for waste that often amounts to as much as half the total weight. In a fish market, the fishman will clean the fish and cut it any way you like. Thus, if you don't want to get involved in cleaning or filleting fish, you don't have to.

No matter how fish has been cut, it can be baked, braised, broiled, fried, poached, sautéed, or steamed. And no matter what cooking method you use, the timing is always exactly the same: ten minutes per inch of thickness! To measure, lay the fish on its side, take a ruler, and determine the thickness of the fish at its thickest point. If you are cooking a rolled fillet, measure the fillet after it has been rolled. Baked fish should be cooked in a 450° F. oven, and poached fish should be timed when the water starts to simmer. Double the cooking time for fish that is cooked frozen. This ten-minutes-an-inch method total cooking time was developed by the Canadian Department of Fisheries and it works for saltwater fish and freshwater fish. It is not applicable to shellfish.

Overcooking is almost the only thing that can go wrong when you prepare fish. But if you use the Canadian method, it won't be overcooked.

There are a limited number of things that can be done with overcooked fish. Probably the best solution, one that also will work with any leftover fish, is to use it in a good recipe for fish cakes, croquettes, or mousse. If you have fish that will taste good cold, overcooked fish may also be used in a salad.

QUICK SOLUTIONS

Fish is too dry

- Serve with a cream sauce, egg-based sauce, melted butter, and/or lemon juice.
- Flake and use in a casserole or salad.

Flavor of fish is too bland

- Sprinkle with herbs, spices, seasoned butter, sautéed almonds, and/or lemon juice.

Fish doesn't flake properly

- Continue cooking.

CHECKLIST FOR NEXT TIME

Problem	Probable Cause
Fish is too dry	– Did you cook it too long? – Was the cooking temperature too high? – Had the fish been frozen?
Poached fish falls apart	– Did you cook it too long? – Did you let the water boil, instead of simmer? – Did you forget to wrap it in cheesecloth (if appropriate) during poaching?
Fish tastes or smells too "strong"	– Did you buy it too far in advance? – Was it less than fresh when you bought it?
Fish is tough or stringy	– Had the fish been frozen? – If frozen, was the fish too poorly wrapped to protect it from drying out? – If frozen, was it kept in the freezer too long?
Breading falls off fried fish	– See chapter on Breading.

FOOD PROCESSORS

Just about everyone who owns a good food processor, and has learned how to use it properly, agrees that it is one of the greatest aids to home cooking to appear in years. If pressed, I think I would rather do without my dishwasher than my food processor. The reason is very simple. With a food processor there are a great many things a person can do quickly and efficiently that formerly were too complicated and time consuming for the average home cook to try. Quenelles, terrines, and marzipan (almond paste) are some of the things that come to mind.

But unless a food processor is used properly, it can cause as many problems as it solves. Some of the problems can be corrected—some cannot.

A distraught young woman approached me at the beginning of a food processor class one day and confessed she was afraid to use her food processor any more because her husband had told her that if she served him "baby food" again he would start eating out—alone. She had not learned how to avoid overprocessing food. I have had other students tell me they were so afraid to use the machine, they had never taken it out of the box. Undeniably, any machine can be dangerous if it is not used carefully and correctly. It's understandable that some people might be concerned about using a food processor to its fullest capacity, or experimenting with it in order to learn how to use it properly, or even using it at all. This is a shame because a food processor is really neither difficult nor complicated to use.

Unfortunately, most food processors do not come with a really good book. But there are some very good books published that provide clear, step-by-step information on what a food processor can do, how it will do it, and even what it cannot do. Different machines work similarly enough to make it possible to use almost any of these books, no matter which machine you own. If you don't already own such a book, buy one. It seems to me that anyone who has invested the considerable amount of money necessary to buy a well-made machine should be willing to invest a few dollars more in order to learn how to use it properly.

The biggest problem most people encounter using the machine is the tendency to overprocess food. It takes only a minute to chop one pound of ground beef correctly. It will take only a few seconds longer to turn the meat into unusable mush. The best way to learn when to stop chopping is to overchop on purpose, once, so you can recognize the point at which the meat was chopped correctly. Set aside a few dollars and buy food you can experiment with. Once you have learned the point at which onions, celery, and nuts, for example, become over-processed, you will avoid the time and expense of having to throw away a completed dish.

It is important to learn in what order food should be added to a food processor. If you want to make chopped egg or tuna salad with raw onion and celery, and you put all the ingredients into the food processor at the same time, the eggs or tuna will indeed be "baby food" by the time the onion and celery are properly chopped. If on the other hand you partially chop the onion and celery and then add the eggs and remaining ingredients, the eggs will not be overchopped when the onion and celery are the right size. Don't make the mistake of waiting until everything is chopped before you add the mayonnaise and season-ings. If you use the food processor to mix them at this point, every-thing will be overchopped.

In order to learn how to avoid overprocessing food, it is vital to get a firm hold on the "on and off" procedure. If you stop the machine and the food is not adequately chopped, you can always turn it back on. But if you don't stop the machine soon enough, you cannot "unpro-cess" the food. I prefer to use the manual on-off method, even when there is a pulse button, because I feel I am in complete control. Most new machines have a pulse button to turn the machine on and off, but there are times when I feel the pulse button doesn't turn the machine off fast enough.

Whether or not overprocessed food can be rescued depends entirely on what food has been overprocessed. Here are some ideas on what to do with overprocessed foods. You probably can think up even more.

Overprocessed food:	Use for:
Fruit	Fruit drink; fruit sauce; jam or jelly; baby food; geriatric food
Mushrooms	Duxelles; add to soup or sauce
Nuts	Nut butters (particularly peanuts)
Shrimp	Shrimp paste
Vegetables	Pureed vegetable dish; gravy and sauce thickener; soup base; baby food; geriatric food

GELATIN

Years ago, any cook who wanted to make a gelatin-based recipe was faced with a task so arduous that she surely must have had second thoughts about including such a dish on a menu. Today both flavored and unflavored gelatin are readily available, so you can make an endless number of inviting dishes for any course in the meal. Properly used, gelatin is a boon to cooking; improperly used, it can lead to all sorts of last-minute disasters.

There are some things guaranteed to cause problems when you use gelatin. If you know what they are to begin with, you should be able to avoid trouble.

Gelatin must be completely dissolved before you can proceed with a recipe. If it is not completely dissolved at the very beginning, your dish will not set properly.

Some fresh or frozen fruits and their juices (pineapple, figs, mangoes, and papayas) have an enzyme that prevents gelatin from setting. However, in canned form, these fruits or their juices can be used successfully with gelatin.

If you add solid food to a gelatin mixture without allowing the gelatin to thicken first, the food will settle at the bottom or, when unmolded, be crowded at the top of your mold.

Be sure to drain canned fruit or vegetables thoroughly before you add them to a gelatin mixture. If you inadvertently add more liquid than you should, your dish will not gel. On the other hand, if you measure carefully, you can substitute fruit or vegetable juice for the liquid called for in a recipe.

Rinse your mold in cold water and coat it with a thin film of tasteless vegetable oil before you fill it. Whenever possible, use a plastic or thin flexible metal mold. It can make unmolding simpler than it is when you use a rigid mold. Leave enough time for your dish to set properly. Depending on the shape of the dish and the quantity of food used, a gelatin dish normally will take anywhere from three hours to overnight to set properly. In an emergency, you can speed up the setting time by using a metal mold, by chilling the mold in a dish of ice and water before placing it in the refrigerator, or by substituting two cups of ice cubes for each cup of cold water in the recipe, stirring about three minutes to melt the ice, and then removing the unmelted ice.

If your mold does not gel properly, there really is nothing you can do except serve it as is—or start over.

People worry more about how to unmold a dish than about how to make it in the first place. And unmolding can be very tricky. The first step is to make sure your mold is completely set. When you are ready to unmold it, fill a large bowl or pot with hot, but not boiling, water. Immerse the mold in the hot water to a point just below the rim and hold it there while you count to ten (about ten seconds). Tilt the mold from side to side to ease the gelatin away from the sides of the dish and to let air in. Remove the mold from the water and dry the outside. Run the tip of a small metal spatula or knife around the edge of the gelatin. Place the serving dish over the mold, hold them tightly together with both hands, and invert. If you are very lucky, the gelatin will ease out of the mold and sit squarely on the plate. If it does not, shake gently and use the blunt end of a knife to tap the mold all the way around and on the top. If nothing happens, repeat the entire procedure, but don't immerse the mold in hot water for as long as before.

On the other hand, if too much has happened and you see liquid emerging from the edges of the mold, leave the mold in place and put everything in the freezer for about five or ten minutes. Then start the unmolding procedure again, immersing the mold in hot water only to the count of five.

It is very difficult to unmold anything squarely in the center of a dish. However, if you rinse the serving dish in cold water before you unmold the gelatin, you should be able to ease the food in place. It is also very difficult to unmold a gelatin salad directly onto greens. It is much better to unmold it onto the serving dish and then lift the edges of the gelatin carefully with the blunt end of a spatual and slip greens under it, or to use greens as a garnish around it.

The procedure for unmolding a frozen bombe or Bavarian cream is slightly different. You should remove the mold from the freezer and invert it directly onto a chilled serving dish. Wrap the mold in a very hot damp dish towel. Tap all around and lift the mold off. If the mold doesn't come off, reheat the towel and try again. Return the unmolded dessert to the freezer until about ten minutes before you are ready to serve it.

Never leave unmolding until the very last minute. If you are going to have trouble, you don't want difficulties to arise while guests are sitting at the table. If, despite all precautions, everything comes out in an ungraceful heap, the ingredient you will need most is imagination. Spoon the mess into individual serving dishes and cover your mishap with an appropriate topping. Use whipped cream or one of the following:

"Relished" Russian Dressing   MAKES ABOUT 2 CUPS

1¼ cups mayonnaise (homemade or commercial)
½ cup catsup or chili sauce
2 tablespoons prepared horseradish, drained
2 tablespoons sweet pickle relish, drained
1 tablespoon onion relish, drained
1 teaspoon Worcestershire sauce
1 teaspoon lemon juice
  Few drops hot pepper sauce

Combine all ingredients in bowl and stir to blend well. Cover and refrigerate until serving time.

NOTE: Originally Russian dressing was made with caviar instead of relish. If you happen to have a jar of caviar on hand, substitute it for the relishes for an unusual taste treat. Domestic caviar will do very nicely.

Sour Cream Dressing for Fruit Salads   MAKES ABOUT 1½ CUPS

½ cup dairy sour cream
½ cup mayonnaise (homemade or commercial)
3 tablespoons orange juice or lemon juice
½ cup heavy cream, whipped
  Salt to taste

Combine sour cream, mayonnaise, and orange juice in bowl; stir until well combined. Fold whipped cream into sour cream mixture. Refrigerate until serving time.

Quick Fruited Yogurt Dressing   MAKES 1¼ CUPS

1 container (8 ounces) plain or vanilla-flavored yogurt
3 to 4 tablespoons jam or marmalade
1 teaspoon lemon juice

Combine all ingredients in bowl and beat with wooden spoon to blend. Cover and refrigerate until serving time.

Melba Sauce   MAKES ABOUT 2 CUPS

2 packages (10 ounces each) frozen raspberries,
   thawed
¼ cup currant jelly
2 tablespoons sugar
¼ cup kirsch

Place raspberries in container of blender or food processor and puree. Place jelly and sugar in saucepan and cook over moderate heat, stirring constantly until jelly and sugar have dissolved. Remove pan from heat, add kirsch, and stir. When jelly mixture has cooled, add raspberries and stir well. Cover and refrigerate until serving time.

QUICK SOLUTIONS

Gelatin begins to melt while being unmolded

• Leave gelatin in mold, inverted on plate, and place mold and plate in freezer 5 to 10 minutes. Then follow unmolding procedure again.

Unmolded gelatin does not hold shape

• Divide into serving portions in the kitchen and garnish with a dressing or sauce.

Gelatin is not fully set

• Place in freezer briefly to speed setting or return to refrigerator until fully set. If it still won't set, divide into serving portions.

CHECKLIST FOR NEXT TIME

Problem	Probable Cause
Gelatin did not set at all	– Did you use too little gelatin? – Did you add too much liquid? – Did you include one of the fresh fruits that prevent gelatin from setting?
Gelatin is not as firm as it should be	– Was the gelatin not quite dissolved before you added it to the rest of the liquid? – Did you add too much liquid? – Did you chill too short a time?
Gelatin refuses to un-mold	– Did you forget to rinse mold in cold water before you filled it? – Did you forget to oil mold? – Did you forget to loosen gelatin around edges? – Did you hold mold in hot water too short a time before unmolding?
Gelatin melts while unmolding	– Did you start to unmold before gelatin was completely set? – Did you hold mold in hot water too long?

INCREASING AND DECREASING RECIPES

If you take a recipe for four and divide it in half because there are only two for dinner, it usually is not very complicated. And often it is just as easy to double a recipe for four so you can feed eight. But increasing or decreasing recipes is not always as simple as it might seem at first glance. And there are some recipes for which the yields cannot be changed at all.

As a general rule, it is better to make two separate batches of cake or bread than to double a baking recipe. And it is also safer to make a full cake or bread recipe, and freeze part of it, than to cut the recipe in half.

The easiest kinds of recipes to increase or decrease are casseroles, sauces, cookies, muffins, cupcakes, most drinks and appetizers, and almost all soups and vegetables. But—and it is a very important "but"—seasoning cannot automatically be increased along with other ingredients. Recently a friend called me to discuss a dinner party she was giving. In the course of our conversation, I learned she was planning to triple a chicken recipe. As we talked, I discovered to my horror that she was going to triple every ingredient in the recipe, including four teaspoons of curry. If, in the end, she had actually put twelve teaspoons of curry in her tripled recipe, the curry flavor would have been so overwhelming she would have had to throw out the entire dish. And, if she had not discovered her mistake until her guests were seated at the table, I have no doubt she would have been very embarrassed (and her guests would have been very hungry).

When it is a question of increasing (or even decreasing) seasoning, the best rule to follow is to ignore all stated amounts for seasoning—and flavor to taste. Add the seasoning slowly and carefully. And remember, under-seasoning is always preferable to over-seasoning. Even in simple recipes where the only seasoning is salt and pepper, don't automatically double the seasoning. It probably will be too much.

When you convert a conventional recipe to a microwave method, be sure to decrease the seasoning (and liquids, too). The speed with which food is cooked in a microwave oven tends to intensify some flavors and eliminates the time necessary for flavors to blend properly.

If anyone were to ask me what piece of kitchen equipment I would most like to see developed, I would not hesitate even a minute. I dream of the day when someone will offer cooks a really good kitchen calculator. Trying to figure out one-third of a half cup of sugar, or three and a half times three-fourths cup of flour, requires a better grasp of mathematics than many of us have. It may seem like a strange concept, but recipes can fail if the cook is weak in the multiplication or division of fractions. When you are increasing or decreasing a recipe, your mathematics must be very accurate.

Cooking in quantity presents more problems than just those encountered in multiplying ingredients:

Remember to include additional preparation time for some ingredients.

Don't overtax kitchen equipment and expect your food processor, blender, or mixer automatically to handle larger quantities.

Be sure you have mixing bowls and pots big enough to handle increased amounts of food.

Consider that you may even need a particularly strong stirring arm to mix food properly when ingredients are substantially increased.

Don't forget to make the proper adjustments in cooking time, particularly if you use a microwave oven where timing is directly related to volume.

And finally, consider your refrigerator space and serving dishes, along with ways to keep large quantities of food hot or properly refrigerated.

The best route to follow when you want to increase a recipe is to think through all the problems you may encounter and then choose your recipe carefully. Stick to dishes that multiply easily, can be made well ahead, and will not require endless hours of preparation.

MEASURING, SUBSTITUTIONS, AND EQUIVALENTS

Many kitchen failures are directly attributable to incorrect measuring. There are occasions when measuring does not have to be exact because it is, after all, a matter of taste that determines how much salt and pepper you use. But some recipes, particularly pastries, are carefully worked-out chemical formulas that must be followed exactly to insure success.

When exact measurements are required, it is important to have the right measuring equipment. Nowhere is this more apparent than in dry and liquid amounts. There is a crucial difference between liquid and dry measuring cups, a fact that is often overlooked, even by experienced cooks. The glass measuring cup that looks like a little pitcher is specially designed to measure liquids. If you fill a cup to the very top with liquid, some of it will spill before you can transfer the liquid to a bowl or saucepan. Therefore, the cup mark on a liquid measuring cup is slightly below the top of the pitcher. On the other hand, dry ingredients like flour and sugar should be filled to the top of the measure and then leveled off with the blunt edge of a knife or spatula. To measure a level cup of a dry ingredient properly you should use the measure that holds an exact cup when full. If you fill the glass-pitcher measure to the top, you will have more than a cupful. And always use the smaller measuring cups, those that hold an exact eighth, fourth, third, or half cup, when your recipe calls for less than a full cup of dry ingredients.

In addition to measuring cups, standard measuring spoons are essential in even a modestly equipped kitchen. A standard tablespoon is not the same as a soup spoon because eating utensils vary in size and capacity. When a recipe calls for a teaspoon of baking powder, it does not mean you can use approximately a teaspoonful. You must be exact if the recipe is to work. Two sets of measuring spoons will make your life even easier and your cooking more accurate. With only one set of measuring spoons available, you will have to dry a spoon, even if it's only been used for water, before you can use it to measure a dry ingredient. You will also have to stop and wash it if you have measured almost anything else. With two sets of spoons available, you will have fewer interruptions.

When you measure a dry ingredient in a measuring spoon, fill the measure by heaping the ingredient in the spoon, then level it off with a spatula or the blunt side of a knife. Liquid ingredients are easier to measure because it's hard to overfill a spoon!

Be sure you understand measuring terminology in a cookbook. "One cup sifted flour" means sift the flour—then measure. "One cup flour, sifted" means measure the flour—then sift. The amount of flour will not be the same. You will also get different amounts from "1 cup chopped nuts" and "1 cup nuts, chopped." There is even a difference in amount, slight though it is, between "1 cup melted butter" and "1 cup butter, melted." Read the list of ingredients carefully when exact measurements count.

Helpful Substitutions

1 teaspoon baking powder	½ teaspoon cream of tartar plus ⅓ teaspoon baking soda
2 tablespoons all-purpose flour	1 tablespoon potato flour
1 cup honey	1¼ cups sugar plus ¼ cup water
⅛ teaspoon cayenne	4 drops hot pepper sauce
1 cup whole milk	½ cup evaporated milk plus ½ cup water or
	1 cup skim milk plus 2 tablespoons melted butter
1 cup light cream	¾ cup milk plus ¼ cup melted butter
1 cup heavy cream	¾ cup milk plus ⅓ cup melted butter
1 cup plain yogurt	1 cup buttermilk
1 cup plain bread crumbs	¾ cup fine cracker crumbs
1 tablespoon flour	1½ teaspoons cornstarch or arrowroot
1 ounce chocolate	3 tablespoons cocoa plus 2 teaspoons shortening

1 cup sour cream	⅓ cup melted butter plus ¾ cup sour milk (To make sour milk, use ¾ cup whole milk plus 2¼ teaspoons lemon juice or 2¼ teaspoons white vinegar. Let mixture stand 10 minutes.)
1 teaspoon lemon juice	½ teaspoon vinegar
1 tablespoon fresh snipped chives	1 teaspoon frozen chopped chives
1 teaspoon dry mustard	2½ teaspoons prepared mustard
1 tablespoon fresh herbs	1 teaspoon dried

Helpful Equivalents

1 cup dry noodles	=	1¾ cup cooked
8 ounces dry spaghetti	=	3½ cups cooked
1 pound fresh mushrooms	=	5 cups sliced
		18 to 20 medium-size whole
1 medium-size orange	=	about 7 tablespoons orange juice
1 medium-size lemon	=	about 2½ tablespoons lemon juice
1 medium-size lime	=	about 2 tablespoons lime juice
1 pound potatoes	=	3 medium-size whole
		2 cups cooked mashed
		3¾ cups sliced
1 pound cabbage	=	4 cups shredded raw
		2 cups cooked
1 pound apples	=	3 medium-size whole
		3 cups sliced
2 medium-size onions	=	1 cup chopped
1 large marshmallow	=	10 miniature
1 cup marshmallows	=	11 to 12 large
2 slices slightly stale bread	=	1 cup soft bread crumbs
12 square graham crackers	=	1 cup graham cracker crumbs
22 saltine crackers	=	1 cup cracker crumbs
¼ pound shelled nuts	=	1 cup chopped
1 envelope unflavored gelatin	=	1 tablespoon (to set 2 cups liquid)
1 pound boneless meat	=	2 cups ground
1 pound all-purpose flour, unsifted	=	4 cups, unsifted
1 pound small shrimp	=	about 50
1 pound jumbo shrimp	=	about 20

MEAT

Whenever I lecture on meat someone is sure to ask me why it is that sometimes a London broil is tender and juicy, and sometimes it tastes like leather. The reason is very simple. London broil is not a cut of meat; it is a way of cooking meat. The cut of meat, as well as the grade, is what determines whether or not meat will be tender.

Essentially all meat is cooked by one of two methods—moist heat or dry heat. When the less tender cuts are cooked by moist, slow heat, the cooking process tenderizes them. But meat that is cooked by dry heat—broiling, roasting, or pan frying—is likely to be tough unless it is tender to begin with or it has been marinated before it is cooked. A top round London broil that is a good grade should be tender. Chuck, often sold as London broil, is almost never tender enough to cook by dry heat. This is true despite the fact that chuck steaks are commonly sold without the caution that they should not be broiled as sirloin or porterhouse steaks are.

The only way consumers can protect themselves from the grief of tough meat is to learn which cuts can be cooked by dry heat and what grade to buy. The front part of the animal (the chuck, or shoulder, end) does the most work as the animal moves about and therefore is the least tender. The rear half, or the round, is pulled along by the front and doesn't have to work quite so hard, so it is more tender than the front. The area along the back is the most tender because it gets a free ride while the animal grazes. This is the loin.

The grade of meat most often sold at retail is USDA Choice. USDA

Prime, the top grade, is one grade higher and is sold largely in specialty meat stores and at really fine restaurants. If the cut of meat you choose is tender, and the grade is either USDA Prime or USDA Choice, you should find that it can be cooked successfully by dry heat. However, although all of the meat you buy is *inspected* by the government to insure that it is free from contamination, not all meat is *graded*. Many supermarkets sell what is called "house brand" meat which, in plain language, means the meat has been inspected but not graded. Much of this meat corresponds in quality to USDA Good, one grade below USDA Choice, and often is not tender enough to cook by dry heat. When meat has been graded, it usually is advertised as such. The consumer can safely assume that if the label does not say USDA Choice or USDA Prime, the meat is probably ungraded. Don't be taken in by ads or labels that use the words "choice" or "prime" as adjectives. If these words indicate a grade, the initials USDA must also appear.

All too many advertisements for meat tell the consumer, somewhat gratuitously, that the meat is "U.S. Government Inspected." Clearly it is the hope of the advertiser that the consumer will think this statement means the meat is exceptionally fine. But, since all meat that crosses state lines is U.S. government inspected, and all other meat is state inspected, this statement should tell the consumer, instead, that the advertiser has nothing special he can say about the quality of his meat, and that, in addition, the meat probably has not been graded or is of a low grade. If the meat had been given a high grade, the advertiser surely would say so. When I see an advertisement that says nothing more than the fact that the meat has been "government inspected," I make a point of buying my meat elsewhere.

Two areas that create confusion when buying or cooking meat are how much to buy and how long to cook it. How much to buy depends on many things: the size of the portions you want to serve, how much other food will be served with the meat, and, most important, how much waste there is in a specific cut. When you serve a completely boneless cut that has no covering of fat, like veal cutlet, you usually need only about one-fourth of a pound per person. On the other hand, if you serve a very bony cut, like spare ribs, you probably will need about three-fourths of a pound or more per person. Therefore it is very important to inspect meat when you buy it and determine how much of what you are buying is edible and how much is bone or fat.

It is far more complicated to figure out how long meat should be cooked. The less tender cuts of meat must be cooked until they are fork tender. Timing depends on the size of the pieces of meat being cooked (pot roast takes longer to cook than beef stew) and on how tender the meat is to begin with. When meat is cooked by dry heat, cooking time often depends on personal preference and on the tenderness of the cut. Most meat thermometers encourage people to cook meat longer than may be necessary, and this is particularly true for lamb, which is absolutely delicious served pink and juicy. Veal is young meat and is therefore usually tender to begin with. It almost never needs to be cooked as long as most recipes suggest. Steaks and chops should be cooked exactly to the point of doneness you want them to be when you eat them, and they should be served immediately. Roasts, on the other hand, should be cooked to a point five to ten degrees below where you want them and then allowed to stand fifteen to twenty minutes to "set" while they finish cooking outside the oven. Allowing a roast to set will make carving an easy job. Fresh pork should be cooked to an internal temperature of 170° F. On the other hand, a ham labeled "fully cooked, ready-to-eat" needs nothing more than heating, and may even be eaten cold.

There are many kinds of meat that can be frozen and then cooked without having to be defrosted first. Steaks and chops are best when they have been slightly defrosted before they are cooked. The extra cooking time necessary depends on the thickness of the meat. A frozen roast will require one-third more cooking time than the same roast requires if it is not frozen.

When the only meat you have on hand is a less tender cut or grade and unexpected company calls, there are several things you can do. If time permits, marinate the meat. The wine or vinegar in a marinade softens the fibers and tenderizes the meat. If it is a good marinade, it will also flavor the meat. If you have a food processor or a meat grinder, you can grind the meat and make fancy meatballs or hamburgers. Grinding also tenderizes meat. Commmercial tenderizers can be used, but although they can indeed make the meat somewhat more tender, they may not do much for its flavor. If you want to speed up the effect of marinating, cut the meat into thin slices, across the grain, marinate it for just thirty minutes, and then use the meat in a stir-fry recipe. You can also cut the meat into strips and use it effectively in *boeuf bourguignon*, but don't try to use it in beef Stroganoff because that recipe should be made with meat that is already tender.

If you have cooked a roast that is not as well done as you would like it to be when you are ready to eat, you can serve a few of the more well done slices from each end and return the balance of the roast to a hot oven, where it will continue to cook while you start eating. You can also place slices of rare meat under the broiler for quick cooking. This method also works very well when people who are sharing the same roast are divided in their preference for rare or well done meat.

However, if you had planned to serve meat rare and overcook it, there is no way you can reverse the results. You will have to eat the meat well done and remember to watch your timing more carefully next time. Utterly overcooked meat tends to be dry, stringy, tough, and difficult to carve. It also may not have as much flavor as less thoroughly cooked meat. When you are faced with this kind of disaster, the best solution is to slice the meat as best you can in the kitchen and serve it with a well-flavored gravy or a sauce spooned over it. If time allows, you can cube the meat and sauté it quickly with vegetables and something flavorful like garlic and onions. Probably the most well-known dish that can be made with overcooked meat is hash.

I bumped into an acquaintance in the supermarket one day, and knowing I wrote cookbooks, she asked me for a menu suggestion. As hard as I tried, I could not come up with a suggestion that appealed to her. She finally confessed that the reason she had a problem was that her husband and children refused to eat any meat except steaks and chops. No wonder she was having trouble figuring out an original menu! The more expensive meat becomes, the more important it is to learn about unfamiliar cuts and to find reliable recipes that explain how to cook them. How sad it is that this particular family never learned that there are many cuts of meat every bit as delicious as steaks and chops. As long as you choose the correct cut of meat for your cooking method, you should be able to serve many different kinds of meat, each of them a pleasure to eat.

Flavorful Meat Marinade   MAKES ABOUT 2 CUPS

½ cup olive oil or peanut oil	1 small onion, sliced
½ cup dry sherry or vermouth	1 small carrot, sliced
½ cup soy sauce	2 bay leaves
1 tablespoon lemon juice	6 peppercorns
2 cloves garlic, finely minced	½ teaspoon thyme

Combine all ingredients in glass jar with screw top. Shake jar vigorously until ingredients are well combined. Place meat in shallow glass baking dish, pour marinade over, turning to coat all sides. Cover and refrigerate several hours, turning often. For added flavor, brush meat with marinade during cooking.

Beef Sauté   SERVES 4

1 onion, sliced
1 green pepper, cut into 1-inch squares
½ pound mushrooms, sliced
1 clove garlic, minced
3 tablespoons butter
2 cups cooked diced beef
1 can (8 ounces) tomato sauce or 1 cup beef gravy
½ cup dry vermouth
¼ teaspoon tarragon
Salt and freshly ground pepper to taste
Unsalted peanuts for garnish

In large skillet sauté onion, green pepper, mushrooms, and garlic in butter until onion is transparent. Add beef, tomato sauce, vermouth, tarragon, salt, and pepper. Stir well and simmer about 10 minutes. Garnish with peanuts and serve over cooked noodles or rice.

Dilled Meat Roll   SERVES 4

1 large onion, finely chopped
2 tablespoons butter
1 pound lean ground beef or lamb or 1 pound
    lean beef or lamb on hand, properly ground
⅔ cup seasoned dry bread crumbs
3 tablespoons chopped fresh dill
    Salt and freshly ground pepper to taste
1 cup dairy sour cream
2 egg yolks, lightly beaten
4 phyllo leaves
¼ cup melted butter (about), divided

Lightly grease cookie sheet. Preheat oven to 325° F. Sauté onion in butter about 3 minutes. Add meat and sauté until lightly browned. Drain off excess fat and set meat mixture aside. Combine bread crumbs, dill, salt, pepper, sour cream, and egg yolks. Mix well. Add reserved meat and onion and mix to combine. Place meat on large piece of waxed paper and shape into a rectangle approximately 12 x 2½ inches. Place 1 phyllo leaf on damp kitchen towel, cover with second phyllo leaf, and brush top surface with melted butter. Cover with remaining 2 phyllo leaves and brush top surface with melted butter. Transfer rectangle of meat onto phyllo leaves, about ½ inch in from long edge of leaves. Fold that edge over meat; fold leaves at both short edges over meat; pick up towel along folded long edge and roll meat over toward other long edge of phyllo leaves to enclose meat completely. Brush surface of leaves with melted butter on all sides and place on prepared cookie sheet. Bake 15 to 20 minutes until phyllo leaves are lightly browned on top. Turn roll over with spatulas and bake an additional 15 to 20 minutes until phyllo leaves are crisp and flaky. Serve with hollandaise sauce.

QUICK SOLUTIONS

Roast is too rare when you are ready to eat

- Serve slices from each end of roast and return balance of roast to a hot oven to finish cooking.
- Slice meat and broil until done.

Meat is too well done

- Slice in kitchen and serve with gravy or sauce.
- Cube or dice and sauté with vegetables.
- Grind up and make hash.

Meat is frozen when you are ready to cook

- NEVER immerse meat in warm water.
- Defrost meat in microwave oven if possible.
- Cook frozen, but adjust cooking time.

CHECKLIST FOR NEXT TIME

Problem   Probable Cause

Meat is too well   — Did you forget to weigh meat before you estimated
done   cooking time?
    — Did you cook meat at too high a temperature?

Meat is too rare   — Did you forget to weigh meat before you estimated
    cooking time?
    — Did you cook meat at too low a temperature?

Meat is tough   — Did you buy a low grade of meat?
    — Did you buy the wrong cut of meat for your cook-
    ing method?

Meat lacks flavor   — Did you buy a low grade of meat?
    — Did you overcook meat?
    — Did you forget to season meat properly?

Meat is not juicy   — Did you buy a low grade of meat?
    — Did you salt meat prior to broiling instead of add-
    ing salt after meat was cooked?
    — Did you overcook meat?

PASTA

Some important foods have the distinction of having an entire museum devoted to them, and pasta is one that has been so honored. The Museo Storico deli Spaghetti is located in Pontedassio, Italy. It houses, among other things, an impressive collection of books, documents, and works of art, all devoted to the long history of pasta in Italy, dating from the thirteenth century.

Thomas Jefferson brought home a spaghetti die after his diplomatic service in Europe, and as president, he served pasta at the White House. And when English dandies retured from the Grand Tour during the eighteenth century with their newly acquired manners and customs, they were called "macaronis." (Remember the lines from "Yankee Doodle Dandy"?)

Although the casual way in which we eat pasta today may bear little resemblance to the pasta-eating customs of the eighteenth and nineteenth centuries, when it was a luxury, the pasta itself has not changed very much. It is still made, as it was then, with flour, salt, water, and the optional addition of eggs and oil.

You have four choices when you want to serve pasta. You can make it yourself, which is a lot of work, but worth the effort; you can buy fresh pasta if you are lucky enough to live near a shop that sells it; you can buy imported dry pasta; or you can buy any one of a wide assortment of domestic dry pastas. Aside from the considerable differences in taste, the only difference in cooking methods between fresh and dry pasta is the length of cooking time required. Fresh pasta takes only three to five minutes to cook; dry pasta usually takes eight to twelve minutes. Timing depends on which of the approximately one hundred fifty varieties of pasta you are cooking, and on whether you prefer it *al dente* (firm, literally "to the tooth") or somewhat softer.

More often than not, pasta, combined with other food, is served as a main dish in the United States. It also is frequently served as an accompaniment to the main dish in place of potatoes or rice. However, in Europe, and particularly in Italy, pasta is more likely to be served as course is to whet the appetite, not satisfy it. Of course there are some pasta dishes, such as lasagne, that are served as a main course in Italy, as they are here, but most of the time pasta is served as the preliminary to a meal, rather than as the main attraction.

The most important requirement for cooking pasta properly is a very large pot. Packages of dry pasta usually call for four quarts of water to one pound of uncooked pasta. Most Italian cookbooks recommend using six quarts of water, which is the method I prefer. The pasta should be put in a pot of rapidly boiling salted water to which about one tablespoon of oil has been added. The addition of oil helps to prevent the pieces of pasta from sticking to each other. The pasta should be boiled, uncovered, until it has reached the doneness that suits your taste. Stir only if absolutely necessary to prevent sticking, and then do so very gently with a fork rather than a spoon. Determining when pasta is done requires frequent tasting toward the end of the cooking time. When it is done, it should be drained immediately and placed in a warm bowl, then tossed with seasoned butter or oil, or topped with sauce. Contrary to popular belief, cooked pasta should not be rinsed in cold water. This procedure cools it off and makes it sticky.

Pasta must be cooked until the taste of raw flour has been eliminated. From that point on, pasta should be cooked to suit your taste, but not cooked to the point where it becomes mush. When it is cooked prior to being combined with other food in a casserole, cooking time should be reduced so the pasta will not overcook when the casserole is baked in the oven. Strangely enough, cookbooks and magazines abound with recipes that tell you to combine cooked pasta, cooked meat, and cooked sauce, mixed or layered in a casserole, then cook an additional forty-five minutes to an hour in the oven. When all the food in a casserole is already cooked, there is no reason to cook it in the oven beyond the point where the food is fully heated, the flavors blended, the sauce thickened if necessary, and the cheese melted. Overcooking can destroy the texture of the food, turn seasoning bitter, and certainly waste energy. If you check a casserole while it is baking, you may find it is ready to eat sooner than you had been led to believe from the recipe.

When pasta is undercooked, the remedy is simple enough. Just return it to a pot of boiling water and cook it a little longer. When pasta is overcooked, the best solution is to throw it away and start over. Since pasta can be cooked quickly, there is no logical reason to struggle with a way to rescue what is essentially not worth saving. This is also true if your pasta is stuck together in a miserable gluey mess. Next time, remember to place it in rapidly boiling water and add oil to the water when you cook it.

Fresh pasta is best when it is cooked as soon as possible after it has been made. When this is not possible, it should be stored in an airtight container in the refrigerator or freezer. Leftover cooked pasta can also be frozen, ready to combine with other food when you want to make a quick emergency casserole.

Neither fresh nor dry pasta should ever be cooked in a pressure cooker, and although they can be cooked in a microwave oven, there really is no point because there is no time saving. However, if you have leftover pasta you want to reheat, microcooking is the ideal method. It can be heated quickly without water, and it will come out of the microwave oven hot and moist.

Pasta has more nutritional value and fewer calories than are generally attributed to it. When it is cooked properly and eaten in moderation, there is no reason why it should not appear frequently on the family menu. It is, after all, a food that is almost disaster-proof.

PIE CRUSTS

There are a surprising number of good cooks who are willing to try almost any recipe except a pie crust. Without doubt, it takes time and practice to learn how to make a good crust, but if you follow the rules, it is not really that difficult.

When you make a pie or tart crust, the shortening and water must be cold—just the opposite of cake baking. Butter or shortening should come from the refrigerator. The water used should be ice water.

Use a pastry blender or two knives to cut the shortening into the flour. Do not use your fingers, as the warmth of your fingertips will soften the shortening and make the dough (and your fingers) sticky.

Add ice water, one tablespoon at a time. Toss the dough gently with a fork until all the flour is moistened. Be careful not to add too much water or your dough will be tough and the crust may shrink. (Pie dough can also be made in a food processor. Check a good food-processor cookbook for correct ratio of ingredients.)

When the dough is thoroughly mixed, form it into a ball, flatten the ball, wrap it in waxed paper or plastic wrap, and place it in the refrigerator to chill for about one hour. If the dough is not properly chilled you won't be able to roll it out without adding extra flour, and the addition of too much extra flour will make the pastry dry and crumbly. Dough that is the correct temperature for rolling should be firm, but should "give" slightly when you press a finger in it. It should not be sticky. In order to get it just right and not too hard for rolling, it may be necessary to allow the dough to stand at room temperature briefly when it is removed from the refrigerator.

Making the dough is the easiest part. Rolling it out properly is what takes practice. Improperly rolled dough can be uneven, tough, sticky, and difficult to handle.

Place the dough on a lightly floured smooth surface (marble is ideal). Flour the rolling pin lightly and place it on the center of the dough. Roll away from your body to within half an inch of the edge of the dough. Use light, even strokes. At this point many people get into trouble because they roll in all directions. Instead of doing that, pick up the dough and turn it a quarter turn. Then, starting from the center as before, roll away from your body. Continue to roll out the dough by lifting it and turning it, rather than rolling it randomly. Roll gently; there is no need to press hard. Keep rolling until the dough is from one-eighth to one-quarter of an inch thick and large enough to fit the pie plate.

To transfer the dough from the surface on which it was rolled to the pie plate, place the rolling pin at the edge of the dough, lift the edge of the dough over the rolling pin, and gently roll the dough around the rolling pin. (If the rolling pin is held too high, the crust will stretch and break.) Then unroll the pastry into the pie plate, being careful not to stretch the dough. Ease the pastry into place with your fingertips. If you stretch the dough to make it fit, it will shrink during baking.

Should the pastry tear, moisten the tear with a small amount of ice water and press the edges back together.

Trim the edge with a sharp knife or scissors, leaving one extra inch of pastry around the pie plate. If you are making a one-crust pie, fold the extra inch under to build up the edge; then flute or crimp.

If your recipe calls for a prebaked crust, prick the bottom and sides of the crust, line it with aluminum foil, and fill the pie shell with pastry weights, dry beans, or rice. This will prevent the crust from puffing up. Preheat the oven to 450° F. and bake the crust on the middle rack about ten minutes. Remove the foil and weights (save them to use another time), and bake five minutes longer.

If you are going to fill an unbaked pie crust, don't prick the crust before you fill it. If you do, the juices will run out. Fill the crust and bake the pie in the lower third of a preheated oven.

If you are making a two-crust pie, moisten the edge of the bottom crust, place top crust over filling, trim edge of top crust to same size as bottom crust, press edges together, and crimp or flute edge if desired.

Juice may also run out of a double crust pie if it is not properly vented. Make four or five holes in top crust and place a piece of uncooked macaroni upright in each hole. Remove the macaroni before serving.

Place a strip of aluminum foil around the edge of the crust to prevent the edge from overbrowning. Remove the foil during the last fifteen minutes of baking so the edge will brown lightly.

QUICK SOLUTIONS

Edge of crust is burned

- Remove burned edge as neatly as possible. Camouflage the ragged edge with piped whipped cream.

Soggy crust, burned crust

- These are hopeless disasters for which there are no quick solutions. Discard pie and serve another dessert, perhaps fresh fruit on hand or canned fruit from your emergency shelf.

CHECKLIST FOR NEXT TIME

Problem	Probable Cause
Crust too hard or tough	– Did you add too much water? – Did you add too little shortening? – Did you handle the dough too much? – Did you roll the dough too much?
Crust shrinks	– Did you use too much shortening? – Did you stretch pastry in order to make it fit pan?
Unfilled crust puffed and bumpy	– Did you forget to prick crust? – Was air trapped under crust? – Did you bake crust without weights? – Was oven too cool?

Problem	Probable Cause
Juices run out of filled crust	– Did you forget the bottom crust should not be pricked if you bake it filled? – Did you forget to vent top crust properly? – Did you forget to crimp and seal upper and lower crusts together?
Soggy bottom crust	– Did you forget to cool filling and crust before you put filling in crust?
Crumbly pastry	– Did you add too little water? – Did you add too much shortening?
Edge of crust is over-browned	– Did you forget to cover edge with a strip of foil until the last fifteen minutes of baking?

RICE

One of the interesting things about rice is that there is a genuine cultural difference regarding what is considered to be properly cooked rice. Rice cooked in the oriental manner is somewhat sticky and therefore possible to eat with chopsticks. In the West, we consider that rice is properly cooked when each grain stands apart, although even in our part of the world there is a difference of opinion about whether rice should be firm and slightly crunchy or light and fluffy and somewhat soft.

Rice is a good choice for a company menu because it is easy and quick to prepare, simple to flavor, and economical to serve. Many people who learned to cook a long time ago automatically wash rice before they cook it. And there probably are new cooks who do it too because that is the way their mothers always prepared rice. This is a shame, because rice is a very nutritious food that doesn't need washing, and when it is washed before cooking, some nutrients are washed away.

There are literally hundreds of different kinds of rice, very few of which are available to the average American shopper. Most of them are cooked in much the same way except for slight adjustments in timing. Periodically I come across recipes that call for only long-grain rice or only short-grain rice. This can be very confusing to a cook who has no idea in what way they are different. And if the cook can't find short-grain rice in the market, which sometimes happens, she may not be certain how to proceed with a recipe.

Short-grain rice often is used in puddings or soup, but there is no reason why one kind of rice cannot be substituted for the other, although short-grain rice may take slightly longer to cook than long-grain rice. Brown rice has more nutrients than white rice. It requires more water and a somewhat longer cooking time than white rice. Wild rice is not really rice at all. It is a grass and it does require washing before cooking.

And then there are the instant rices. Since regular rice and converted rice (regular rice with nutrients added) can be cooked quickly, I have never understood the popularity of the more expensive instant or pre-cooked rice. There are also a great many flavored rices on the market, and new ones seem to appear on the shelves almost every day. It is an extraordinarily expensive way to pay for seasoning that you can add at home with the help of a good cookbook or a little imagination.

If you've overcooked rice, or cooked it with too much water, or stirred it vigorously while it was cooking, you probably have a miserable gluey mass. Since rice does not take very long to cook in the first place, my best recommendation is to make a new batch of properly cooked rice. You can use the overcooked rice in other ways: combine it with ground meat, add it to a casserole, mix it with a sauce, use it to stuff peppers, add it to soup, use it in a custard, add it to scrambled eggs or an omelet, or add it to pancake batter. If you have too much to use right away, store it in the freezer.

When rice is cooked ahead of time and must be held for later serving, even properly cooked rice can turn into a sticky mess unless you know what you are about. The best way to hold rice is to place it in a colander, cover it, and set it over simmering water. The steam will keep it warm without making it sticky. This is also the best way to reheat leftover rice.

But all of these problems can be avoided in the first place if you use a foolproof method for cooking rice. With very little effort, you can arrange to have rice done at precisely the minute you want to serve it. The method I recommend above all others is baking. You can get the rice partly ready ahead of time and then pop it in the oven while you are having drinks in the living room. It doesn't need watching, in spite of the fact that it does need careful timing. In an emergency, you can even bake it fifteen minutes, remove it from the oven, and then return it to a preheated oven for final cooking when you are certain dinner will be served soon.

The recipe that follows is even easy to multiply. I made enough to serve sixty people at a wedding once by cooking all of it in the morning in several casseroles and leaving just the last five minutes of cooking until we were ready to serve it. It turned out hot, crunchy, and absolutely perfect.

Herbed Mushroom Pilaf   SERVES 6

2 tablespoons minced onion
1 small clove garlic, minced
3 tablespoons butter, divided
½ pound mushrooms, sliced
1 cup rice
1 can (10¾ ounces) condensed chicken broth,
  undiluted
¼ teaspoon thyme
1 bay leaf
2 drops hot pepper sauce
  Salt to taste
  Snipped parsley for garnish

Preheat oven to 350° F. Sauté onion and garlic in 1½ tablespoons butter about 3 minutes. Add mushrooms and sauté about 5 minutes, or until onion and mushrooms are tender. Place in 1½-quart casserole with rice, broth, thyme, bay leaf, hot pepper sauce, and salt. Cover and bake about 20 minutes, or until all liquid has been absorbed. Remove bay leaf, stir in remaining 1½ tablespoons butter with fork, and garnish with parsley.

You can, if you like, add pignola nuts to this recipe.

From *Fresh Ideas with Mushrooms*, © 1978, *The Benjamin Company, Inc.* used with permission.

SAUCES
AND
GRAVY

Sauce making and *haute cuisine* are almost synonymous, which may be the reason some cooks quake at the mere thought of making a sauce. This can be pretty silly when you realize these same cooks often don't hesitate to make gravy (which, after all, is a sauce) or to make the base for a soufflé or cream puffs (which involve the same principles as making sauces). If your past sauce making has been tried with an elaborate French cookbook in hand, you may have been discouraged before you began because some cookbooks manage to make sauce making seem as complicated as resolving the political differences in the Middle East. But, like almost everything else in cooking, sauce making is neither difficult nor complicated once you understand the principles involved.

White Sauce

I remember only one thing I was taught to make in my sixth-grade home economics class: white sauce. Change the name of that white sauce to béchamel and you have a basic French sauce, a fact no one told me in sixth grade because French was not part of our curriculum. The only real difference is that when we make a white sauce we normally use milk. When the French make a béchamel sauce they often use cream. In either case, butter is melted in a saucepan, an equal amount of flour is added, and the two are stirred over moderate heat two or three minutes to eliminate the taste of raw flour. This makes a smooth paste called a roux. There are several theories about how to add liquid to the roux in order to achieve a smooth sauce. I add cold liquid very slowly, stirring constantly. If you are nervous, heat the liquid before you add it to the roux. If you are very, very nervous, either make the sauce in a double boiler or remove the saucepan from the heat and add the hot liquid off the heat. Return the saucepan to low heat and keep stirring (and don't let anything distract you) until the sauce has thickened. If you elect to add liquid off the heat, it will take longer for the sauce to thicken.

A thin white sauce is made with one tablespoon each of butter and flour for each cup of liquid. A medium-thick sauce requires two table-spoons of butter and flour, a thick sauce three tablespoons of butter and flour. Add seasoning and the sauce is complete. Salt and white pepper are the traditional seasoning. Although the flavor of white pepper is not very different from the flavor of black pepper, black pepper is not used because it tends to look like flecks of dirt in a white sauce.

Once you have learned to make a simple basic béchamel sauce you have the basis for an endless number of other sauces. Add grated cheese and you have a Mornay sauce. Add mustard and you have *sauce moutarde*. Change the milk or cream to stock and you have a velouté sauce. There are literally hundreds of sauces you can make.

One of the nicest things about a béchamel is that it is relatively hardy. Unless you do something terrible to it, like boiling it, there's very little that can happen to destroy it. If it gets too thick, you can always add more liquid—very gradually. If it gets too thin, add *beurre manié* (see page 97). If it somehow manages to develop lumps, put it in a blender. In the unlikely event it should separate, add boiling water, one tablespoon at a time, and stir like crazy. You can refrigerate it, freeze it, or keep it warm in the top of a double boiler. If you have to hold the sauce for any length of time before serving, float a pat of butter on top of the sauce, or butter a piece of waxed paper and place it on the sauce, buttered side down. This will prevent skin from forming on the surface.

As with all cooking, the important thing to remember about a white sauce is that the quality of the ingredients used determines the quality of the final product. If you make a white sauce with margarine, water, and ground pepper that is past its prime, the result may be akin to tasteless glue. If, instead, you use butter, cream, and freshly ground pepper, the sauce will be an asset to any meal.

Whether or not you want to make a thin, medium-thick, or thick white sauce depends on how you plan to use it. Thin sauce is used as a base for creamed soup, as a dessert sauce, or as a coating. Medium-thick sauce is used in casseroles or in such dishes as chicken à la king, lobster Newburg, and filled crepes. Thick sauce can be spooned sparingly over meat, or it can be used as a binding agent for croquettes, as a thick food coating, or as the base of a soufflé. The potentials for using a béchamel sauce to resolve cooking disasters are almost without limit. Puree overcooked vegetables, add a thin béchamel, and you have soup. Cut up leftover chicken, add peas, mushrooms, and a medium-thick sauce, and you suddenly have enough food for unexpected guests. Use tuna fish with a thick sauce to make inexpensive croquettes when the food budget is thin.

Brown Sauce

White sauces are close to being a standard ingredient in many American dishes, but brown sauces are less commonly used. This is undoubtedly so because a brown sauce takes considerably more time to make than a white sauce, even though it is certainly easy enough to make.

When a French chef talks about making a brown sauce, he is speaking of a genuinely complicated, time-consuming procedure in which he is making a demi-glace, a highly concentrated sauce to be used as a base for a wide range of derivative sauces. However, the home cook can make a perfectly acceptable brown sauce without taking a week off from work to accomplish it.

The basic principle of making a roux to which a liquid is added is the same for both white and brown sauces. But a brown sauce requires additional steps. Before flour is added to the fat, you put in finely chopped vegetables, such as onions and carrots. They are cooked until lightly browned. Then the flour is added and cooked five to ten minutes, or until it begins to turn nut brown, making a brown roux. Brown stock is added, it is brought to a boil, the heat is reduced, the mixture is allowed to simmer about an hour, and finally it is strained.

As with béchamel, brown sauce serves as a basis for many other sauces. It depends on what you add. If you add Madeira wine, you have a Madeira sauce. Add white wine, tomato paste, shallots, and mushrooms, and it's a *sauce chasseur*. A brown sauce plus onion, white wine, vinegar, and mustard provides a *sauce Robert*.

If you have already learned how to make a smooth roux, it is hard to imagine what could go wrong with a brown sauce. The one possible exception might be if you leave it simmering on a back burner while you go shopping and then get caught in a traffic jam on the way home.

More often than not, brown sauces are used to dress up a main dish and are served sparingly over meat, fish, or chicken. Sometimes they are also used as part of a recipe for a dish like veal chasseur.

If you want to keep brown sauce on hand to use in an emergency, make it ahead of time and store it in the freezer. It will keep very well.

Gravy

There are many good reasons for making gravy. When it is smooth and well flavored, it is a welcome addition to many meals. Some foods, such as the white meat of chicken or turkey, are relatively dry even when properly cooked and are enhanced when gravy is served with them. Gravy can be used to dress up leftovers and as a food stretcher. In addition, one very important use for gravy is rescuing overcooked meat (see page 76).

I am genuinely horrified by the number of cookbooks that automatically tell you to put gravy through a strainer to remove lumps. Lumps? Properly made gravy doesn't have lumps. If you don't know how to make a smooth beautiful gravy, take heart. It is easier than you think.

For each cup of gravy, use fat (one tablespoon for thin gravy, two tablespoons for medium-thick gravy), an equal amount of flour, one cup of liquid, seasoning, and a browning agent if desired. If you are making pan gravy, begin by pouring off the fat and reserving it. Leave the drippings and juices in the pan. Place the pan over high heat, add a small amount of liquid, and scrape the pan to loosen the drippings. (This process is called deglazing.) Measure the fat you will need for the amount of gravy you are making and return it to the pan. Reduce the heat (to low), add the flour, and keep stirring until you have a smooth paste. This should take about three minutes, long enough to eliminate the unfortunate taste of uncooked flour. At this point the paste should be smooth; otherwise you will not end up with smooth gravy. Increase the heat slightly (to moderate) and pour some liquid into the pan slowly, just a small amount at a time. (The best liquid to use is stock or canned bouillon with a little dry vermouth or dry sherry.) Stir constantly until all the liquid has been incorporated into the paste and it has rethickened. This is the second stage where you want to be sure there are no lumps. If there are, it is still possible to remove them by stirring vigorously before you add more liquid. Continue to add the liquid, a little at a time, until all of it has been incorporated smoothly. Season the gravy, add the browning agent if desired or necessary, and serve immediately. Whenever you have to reheat gravy, be sure to do it slowly, over low heat, stirring constantly.

Your gravy will be lumpy—

if you use more fat than flour,
if you don't make a smooth lump-free paste of fat and flour,
if you add liquid too quickly or before you have a smooth paste,
if you don't stir constantly. (Don't answer the phone in the middle of making gravy.)

If, in spite of all precautions, your gravy is lumpy, put it in a blender or food processor and process until it is smooth. Then reheat it gently. This is a quicker and more effective method than putting it through a strainer.

Is your gravy too salty? Try adding a small amount of brown sugar or vinegar. Sometimes it helps and sometimes it doesn't. You can also make more gravy (without any salt) and mix it in with the oversalted gravy. The technique of adding slices of raw potato to oversalted food is not recommended for gravy. This only works if you can cook the food long enough for the potatoes to absorb the excess salt—and gravy should not be cooked that long.

Greasy sauce or gravy is a real appetite deterrent. The easiest way to remove excess fat is to skim it off with a spoon. If there is time, you can put the gravy in the refrigerator long enough for the fat to rise to the top and solidify, making it easy to remove. Supposedly, excess fat can be removed with lettuce leaves or ice cubes, but I've never found either method very satisfactory. Sometimes the addition of a small amount of baking soda will make the gravy less greasy. A smooth paste of flour and water can be added to absorb some fat but it will also thicken the gravy so you will probably have to add more liquid, too.

If the gravy that accompanies a stew or casserole is too thin, adding flour directly will result in lumpy gravy. There are several safe methods for thickening gravy or sauce. My favorite method is to add *beurre manié*, a mixture of equal parts of flour and butter. To make it, place flour and butter on a piece of waxed paper and work flour into butter until both ingredients are well combined. Add the *beurre manié* to the thin sauce, a little bit at a time, and stir until the butter is melted and both the butter and flour have been absorbed into the gravy. (Next time you have a few free minutes, make some *beurre manié*, shape it into one-inch balls, and store them in the freezer. You'll always have one right on hand when you need it.)

It is also possible to thicken gravy by making a smooth paste of flour and liquid and adding it to the gravy gradually. If you have potato flakes on hand, or a nice thick puree of leftover vegetables, stir them into the gravy. You can also use cornstarch or arrowroot as thickening agents, instead of flour. However, one tablespoon of cornstarch or arrowroot has the thickening power of two tablespoons of flour, and, like flour, they must be dissolved in liquid before they can be added.

Now, about saving overcooked meat with gravy: meat that is over-cooked is usually dry and tasteless. But most meat is much too expensive to throw away or to feed to the dog, no matter how much you love your pet. To serve a piece of meat that is overdone, remove it from the oven and let it stand for about ten minutes to set while you make some gravy. The standing period is not long enough for the meat to get cold and it will make carving easier. Slice the meat as thin as possible, arrange the slices on a platter, and spoon some gravy (not too much) down the center of the platter. Garnish with snipped parsley or dill and serve the meat in a manner that implies you had intended to serve it this way from the very beginning. Make extra gravy to pass at the table so your guests can add more if they want to—and if the meat is very overcooked, they will want to.

Egg-Based Sauces

The two most popular egg-based sauces are hollandaise sauce and mayonnaise. Both are easy to make if you follow directions precisely. Either can cause untold trouble if you don't.

With both hollandaise and mayonnaise, it is necessary to incorporate oil or butter carefully into egg yolks, adding it slowly enough for the egg yolks to absorb the fat, and for the fat to remain suspended in the emulsion. A friend of mine called me not long ago to tell me her just-made hollandaise sauce was a disaster. I questioned her to find out exactly what she had done. Her error was very simple, and it guaranteed disaster. She had added all the butter to the egg yolks at once, instead of cutting the butter into small pieces and adding one small piece at a time. Since there was no way the egg yolks could absorb all that fat at one time, her hollandaise sauce was doomed to failure.

Both hollandaise sauce and mayonnaise can be made in a blender or food processor, a method that is almost foolproof, but not entirely. I was making mayonnaise in a food-processor class one day, feeling full of assurance and confident nothing could go wrong. The recipe was one I had used many times before. I turned on the food processor and added the oil slowly. The result was a thin creamy liquid that I might have used as a new kind of salad dressing, but that certainly was not mayonnaise. It took me a while to figure out what had gone wrong, but I finally determined that the processor bowl had not been thoroughly dried after washing. The presence of even that slight bit of moisture was enough to keep the mayonnaise from thickening. Now, taking care to use a dry bowl, I almost always make mayonnaise in the food processor. I find the quality of mayonnaise made this way similar to mayonnaise whipped by hand. However, I prefer to make hollandaise sauce in the top of a double boiler rather than in a blender or food processor because I find the double-boiler method makes a thicker, creamier, slightly warmer sauce than the blender or food-processor version.

When you make hollandaise sauce, the egg yolks must be beaten and heated slightly in the top of a double boiler over (not in) gently simmering water. (Don't make it in an aluminum saucepan. The sauce will darken!) If the heat is too high, you will have scrambled eggs. The butter must be whisked into the egg yolks, a little bit at a time. The correct ratio is about two ounces of butter to one large egg yolk. If much more butter is used, the egg yolk will not be able to absorb it. Season the sauce with lemon juice, salt, and pepper. If possible, serve immediately.

It is possible to hold hollandaise sauce for several hours over lukewarm water, if necessary. But be sure not to stand it over hot water; the sauce will curdle. There are two diametrically opposite beliefs about what to do when hollandaise sauce begins to curdle. One theory is to add a tablespoon of cold water and beat like the very dickens. The other theory is to add boiling water instead. I prefer the Julia Child method of adding cold water. It works perfectly for me.

A tablespoon of hot water will solve the problem if hollandaise sauce is too thick. If the sauce is too thin it can be thickened, but it takes more than a minute to do. Rinse a bowl in hot water, dry it thoroughly, put in a teaspoon of lemon juice and a tablespoon of hollandaise sauce, beat hard, and it should begin to thicken. Then add about two teaspoons of sauce and beat until that has thickened. Repeat until all the hollandaise sauce has been thickened.

It is reasonable to assume that very few restaurants have the personnel available to whip up fresh hollandaise sauce everytime someone orders it. So what do they do? They stabilize hollandaise sauce by beating one or two tablespoons of béchamel into the finished hollandaise or by beating a teaspoon of cornstarch into the egg yolks before the butter is added. There is no reason why you can't do the same thing!

Leftover hollandaise sauce can be refrigerated or frozen. When you are ready to use it, heat a small amount very carefully, over gentle heat, adding the balance gradually. Or, place it in a microwave oven and heat it briefly on very low power.

Whether you make mayonnaise in a blender, food processor, electric mixer, or by hand, certain rules apply. The bowl in which the mayonnaise is made should be warm and must be thoroughly dry. The egg yolks are beaten in it, the seasoning is added and mixed in, and then the oil is beaten in, almost drop by drop. By the time about half the oil has been added, the mayonnaise should begin to thicken. When it does, it is safe to add the remaining oil somewhat more quickly. A large egg yolk can absorb a maximum of three-fourths cup of oil.

If the mayonnaise begins to curdle, to separate, or to thin out, the procedure for rescuing it is the same as that for rescuing thinned-out hollandaise sauce. The only difference is that prepared mustard should be substituted for lemon juice.

Mayonnaise cannot be frozen, but it can be kept in the refrigerator for about two weeks.

Both mayonnaise and hollandaise sauce can be used as the basis for a wide variety of other sauces by adding various seasonings. And once you have learned how to make these sauces you can use them to add elegance to almost any meal.

QUICK SOLUTIONS

Sauce is lumpy

• Remove lumps by processing in blender or food processor.

Sauce is too thin

• Add one of the following slowly, stirring constantly:
    beurre manié;
    paste of liquid and flour, cornstarch, potato starch, or arrowroot;
    potato flakes;
    pureed vegetables;
    beaten egg yolks to which a small amount of hot sauce has been added gradually.
• If sauce does not contain milk, cream, eggs, or mustard, it may be possible to thicken it by cooking over high heat, but this will also reduce the amount of sauce.

Sauce is too thick

• Add more warm liquid slowly, stirring constantly.

Egg-based sauce begins to curdle or separate

• Add about 1 tablespoon ice water or boiling water and beat hard with a whisk.

CHECKLIST FOR NEXT TIME

Problem	Probable Cause
Lumps in sauce	– Was the roux too hot? – Did you fail to blend the roux to a completely smooth paste? – Was the liquid added to the roux too quickly? – Was your stirring interrupted?
Sauce too thin	– Did you add too little flour? – Did you add too much liquid? – Did you cook the sauce too short a time?

Problem	Probable Cause
Sauce too thick	– Did you add too much flour? – Did you add too little liquid? – Did you cook the sauce too long? – Did you let sauce stand too long (if prepared ahead of time)?
Butter in sauce separates	– Did you cook sauce too long? – Did you cook the sauce over too high heat?
Sauce becomes watery when heated as part of a casserole	– Did you forget to make sauce extra thick to compensate for any ingredient in casserole that expresses additional liquid as it cooks? – Was casserole covered during baking—allowing moisture to collect under cover—when recipe called for baking uncovered?
"Skin" forms on top of sauce	– Did you forget to put a piece of buttered waxed paper on surface of sauce that is prepared ahead of time?

SEASONING

Ever so often I find myself in a strange kitchen trying to make something as simple as a vinaigrette dressing, frustrated because I can't find the basic ingredients needed to provide good flavor. I don't understand why some people regard such items as peppercorns, garlic, fresh lemons, fresh parsley, good quality paprika, or a small jar of tarragon less important in everyday cooking than sugar, flour, or coffee. Most assuredly, a dish that is worth cooking in the first place is worth seasoning properly. Even the most carefully prepared dish will taste bland and uninteresting if no effort has been made to season it.

Fresh herbs like basil and tarragon usually are not available in the winter and can be difficult to find at any time in a big city. Therefore, unless you have an herb garden on your window sill, it is often necessary to use the dried variety. But parsley, and even dill, can be bought fresh at almost any time of year and, when properly wrapped, can be stored in the refrigerator for as long as a month. I have never been able to discern any flavor in a dried parsley flake. Try a blindfold test sometime. You will never know it has been added to a dish. Parsley flakes may add color, but that's about all. In addition, jars of parsley flakes don't contain parsley stems, and the stems, at least when they are fresh, have more flavor than the leaves. When you buy fresh parsley, wash it well, dry it with paper towels, wrap it in a slightly dampened paper towel, put it in a plastic bag, and store it in the refrigerator. Use the stems to flavor stock, soup, stews, and sauces, and include the stems with the leaves when you make a bouquet garni.

The easiest way to chop a small quantity of parsley is with kitchen scissors. A larger amount of parsley can be chopped beautifully in a good food processor, provided the leaves are thoroughly dried before you process them. The aroma of freshly chopped parsley is very special.

When you need an herb that is not available in fresh form, buy the smallest-size jar available and keep the jar tightly closed and away from the heat of the stove. Neither spices nor herbs remain potent very long, and when they deteriorate, they lose both flavor and aroma. Therefore it is better to pass up the very large jars of dried herbs available in most supermarkets unless you feel reasonably certain you can use them up within about a month—an unlikely prospect unless you are planning to feed an army.

Garlic powder and onion powder fall in the same unfortunate category as parsley flakes. Even worse are garlic salt and onion salt. It is a simple matter to keep fresh onions and garlic on hand, and the wonderful flavor they provide doesn't remotely resemble the flavor of the white stuff that comes in jars. When you use onion salt or garlic salt you lose the opportunity to control the exact amount of salt you want to add to a dish. And when you use either the salt or the powder you usually end up with a dish that tastes uncomfortably like the food offered at the local "greasy spoon." For people who like garlic, the aroma of fresh garlic is an enormous appetite enhancer. But I am willing to bet no one ever entered a kitchen, sniffed the air appreciatively, and said "Oh my, that garlic powder smells delicious!"

Fresh lemons are also easy to keep on hand. If you have not developed the habit of using lemon juice as a flavoring agent, you will be surprised at how many ways you can use it to improve the flavor of food and, when necessary, as a replacement for salt in a low-sodium diet. Almost any vegetable you cook will benefit from a squeeze or two of fresh lemon juice. Some meat, like veal cutlets, most fish, many sauces, and certainly salad, all benefit as well. There is a small, inexpensive, plastic gadget you can insert in a lemon that will extract juice quickly and easily. When I need fresh lemon juice, I simply reach in the refrigerator, remove a lemon that has the "juicer" inserted in it, and squeeze. No effort, no fuss, no mess. Next time you serve broccoli, squeeze lemon juice over it instead of using lots of butter. You will be surprised how delicious it will taste.

Any recipe that calls for pepper will taste better with freshly ground pepper than with preground pepper. All you need is a pepper mill and a box of peppercorns. Freshly ground pepper has an incomparable flavor. Use it in cooking and use it at the table. It's a habit worth developing.

The paprika found on the shelves of most supermarkets is almost always the domestic variety. If you want to use paprika as a coloring agent only, this kind will serve very well. But if you also want the paprika you use to have real flavor, you will have to buy imported paprika. I have found Hungarian is the easiest to buy and probably the best flavored. A good quality paprika will add both flavor and eye appeal to many dishes. I always use it liberally when I am roasting a chicken or turkey; it provides a golden glow to the skin. Paprika will do much the same thing if you add it to breading crumbs. For that matter, it is a helpful addition to almost any dish that is bland in either flavor or color.

In the summer, when fresh basil and tarragon are often available, they can be used to provide exceptionally fine aroma and flavor in salads and salad dressings. Basil, along with a dash of sugar, is a wonderful addition to almost any tomato dish. Tarragon, combined with lemon juice and fresh pepper, can be used so successfully to flavor foods like chicken and fish that you won't even miss the salt if you are on a salt-free diet.

If you like curry, it is worth shopping around to search out a good curry. Actually curry is usually a combination of cardamon, cloves, coriander, cumin, dill, fenugreek, ginger, mace, pepper, and turmeric. This combination varies considerably from one manufacturer to another, and some mixtures can be pretty terrible. Indian cooks mix their own curry, which is a good idea if you use curry often enough. When you add curry to a recipe, start with less than the recipe calls for and gradually add more, tasting as you go along, until you get exactly the flavor you want. Nothing can be done to correct a dish that has too much curry in it.

Sometimes you can rescue a dish that has too much salt in it; sometimes you cannot. One thing you might try is to cook more food (without any salt), add it to the dish that is oversalted, and mix well. When that does not seem like a viable option you can add potatoes, continue cooking until the potatoes have absorbed some of the excess salt, discard the potatoes, and serve the dish. If your dish cannot be cooked further, the potato method won't work. In that case you can add a small amount of brown sugar and/or a small amount of vinegar. This may prove helpful, but you can't be sure it will do the trick until you try. In the long run it really is safest to add salt carefully. You can always add more at the table.

Once you begin to understand how much difference good seasoning can make in the final appeal of food, you might consider buying a good book on herbs and spices. It will help you learn the many ways you can use them, and give you the courage to experiment with new flavors and tastes.

Although intelligent seasoning can be used to help improve a dish that has not turned out very well, proper seasoning really should be viewed as an integral part of good cooking rather than a means of hiding bad cooking.

SOUFFLES

Food fads come and go and as a result there are periods when everyone seems to be serving the same dish. One season, it's quiche; the next, crepes; the next, fondue. But soufflés have been around for a very long time and undoubtedly are here to stay. And with good reason. A properly made soufflé is always a pleasure to eat, and since there are an almost endless number of different foods that can be used to flavor a soufflé, it has a place at almost any meal.

Inexperienced cooks are inclined to view a soufflé as complicated and somewhat risky. But soufflés are really not complicated to make, and the risk can be reduced once you understand the basic principles of soufflé making. It is even possible to make a soufflé that will rise a second time when it is reheated or to make one as much as a month in advance and freeze it.

The base of a standard soufflé is a simple white sauce to which something is added, such as chocolate, cheese, spinach, or crab meat. Egg yolks are added to thicken the base further, and then beaten egg whites are folded into the mixture. This mixture is carefully spooned into a well-greased, straight-sided dish and baked in the center of a preheated oven. If you know how to make a white sauce, beat egg yolks into a hot mixture, beat and fold in egg whites (all of which are covered in this book in the appropriate sections), then you already know the basics of making a soufflé.

Although it certainly is true you cannot open and close an oven door at will while a soufflé is baking without causing it to fall, and you cannot prepare a traditional soufflé very much ahead of time, soufflés are not nearly as fragile as many people think they are. You can, for example, prepare a traditional soufflé as long as an hour before you plan to bake it, cover it with a big pot, and set it in a draft-free spot waiting to go into the oven. Once you know that, you have eliminated the need to rush into the kitchen to whip your egg whites while everyone else is enjoying drinks and hors d'oeuvre. Despite rumors to the contrary, you can walk around the kitchen while the soufflé is baking, and you can even open the oven door, carefully, to see if the soufflé is done.

A traditional soufflé is often served slightly runny in the center. If you don't want it to be runny, then you must bake it a few minutes longer. A collar is often put around a soufflé dish because a properly made soufflé will rise well above the dish, and if it is not supported as it rises, it will break apart. The soufflé must be served the minute it comes out of the oven. It cannot sit on the table waiting in the same way a casserole or a roast can be left waiting, because it will fall.

If you would like to prepare a soufflé well ahead of time, it can be done. The texture will be slightly different, but the soufflé will still be light, airy, puffy, and delicious. You have two choices. The first method is to make a soufflé and keep it, unbaked, in the freezer. Then, whenever you choose, thaw before baking, bake in the usual manner, and serve promptly. The alternative is to make a soufflé in the morning, bake it in a pan of water, remove it from the oven, allow it to cool completely (and deflate), then return it to the oven thirty minutes before you want to serve it, and watch it rise a second time! And if you make the double-rising soufflé in a ring mold, you can even remove it from the mold before serving, although this does tend to deflate it somewhat. If you do make it this way, it's a good idea to serve the soufflé with a sauce. It will look better and the sauce will add flavor.

You will find slight differences in the amounts of ingredients used, depending on the preparation method you select. The following chart shows the different amounts used for the three methods of soufflé preparation. By following the instructions in the recipes at the end of this section, you can adapt your favorite soufflé recipes to any of the three methods. Flavorings are omitted from the chart, since they are used in the same amounts no matter which method is used. Each soufflé is baked in a two-quart soufflé dish and serves six to eight people.

	Traditional Soufflé	Double-Rising Soufflé	Frozen Soufflé
Butter	3½ tablespoons	4 tablespoons	2 tablespoons
Flour	4½ tablespoons	8 tablespoons	6 tablespoons
Liquid	1½ cups	1⅓ cups	1½ cups
Egg yolks	6	6	5
Egg whites	7 or 8	6	7

The sauce base of a double-rising soufflé is thicker than the base of a traditional soufflé. It is cooked until it reaches an almost dough-like consistency, and then the egg yolks are beaten in, one at a time. Another major difference between the double-rising soufflé and the others is that the dish in which the soufflé is cooked is placed in a pan of hot water during baking, which almost creates a steam bath for the soufflé. It is not necessary to place a collar around a double-rising soufflé because it will not rise as high as a traditional soufflé.

The big difference between a soufflé to be frozen and the other soufflés is in the way the base is made. The flour and any other dry ingredients are combined, liquid is added, the mixture is brought to a boil, and then butter is added. From that point on, procedures remain the same, except that the soufflé is not baked before freezing. A suggestion: To avoid tying up a soufflé dish in the freezer, line the dish with aluminum foil before you fill it, freeze the soufflé, and then lift it out of the dish. Wrap the frozen soufflé carefully and store it in the freezer. You can now put your soufflé dish back in the cupboard. When you are ready to cook the frozen soufflé, simply unwrap it, grease the soufflé dish, and slip the soufflé back into the dish to thaw before cooking.

If you want to make a traditional soufflé you will find a good assortment of recipes in standard cookbooks. Just be sure to choose a recipe that has clear and precise instructions.

If you would like to make either a double-rising soufflé or a soufflé you can freeze, try one of the recipes that follow. But if you serve either of these soufflés to company, be prepared for skepticism on the part of your guests who may not be willing to believe you really made the soufflé long before they arrived.

Double-Rising Orange Soufflé   SERVES 8

1 tablespoon butter, softened
2 to 3 tablespoons sugar
4 tablespoons sweet butter
½ cup all-purpose flour
1 cup light cream
6 eggs, separated
8 tablespoons sugar, divided
7 tablespoons freshly squeezed orange juice
3 tablespoons curaçao
   Grated rind of 2 medium-size oranges
½ teaspoon cream of tartar

Liberally grease 2-quart soufflé dish with 1 tablespoon softened butter. Sprinkle 2 to 3 tablespoons sugar into dish to coat sides and bottom. Tilt dish from side to side so sugar clings to buttered surface; turn upside down and tap lightly to remove excess sugar. Preheat oven to 350° F. and set kettle of water on to boil. Melt 4 tablespoons butter in medium-size saucepan. Add flour and stir to form smooth paste. Cook 2 to 3 minutes. Add cream slowly and cook over moderate heat, stirring constantly, until mixture thickens. Lower heat and continue to cook, beating constantly with wooden spoon, until mixture is of dough-like consistency and comes away from sides and bottom of saucepan. Transfer mixture to large mixing bowl. Beat in egg yolks, one at a time, making sure each yolk is thoroughly incorporated before adding the next one. Beat in 7 tablespoons sugar, 1 tablespoon at a time. Mix in orange juice and curaçao, 1 tablespoon at a time. Add grated orange rind and stir. Place egg whites in large bowl, add cream of tartar, and beat until soft peaks form. Sprinkle in remaining tablespoon sugar and continue beating until stiff peaks form. Stir 2 heaping tablespoonfuls of beaten egg whites into soufflé base and mix well to lighten base. Fold in remaining egg whites. Spoon mixture into prepared soufflé dish. Set dish in large shallow pan. Place on center shelf of oven. Pour enough boiling water in pan to come halfway up side of soufflé dish. Bake 40 to 50 minutes or until lightly browned on top. Test after 40 minutes by inserting cake tester or toothpick into side of soufflé; if the tester comes out dry, soufflé is done. If tester has any batter on it, or is sticky, another 5 to 10 minutes of baking is necessary. When done, remove from oven and serve immediately, or set aside to cool completely.

To reheat, preheat oven to 350° F. Place soufflé dish in shallow baking pan. Place pan on center shelf of oven and pour in enough boiling water to come halfway up side of soufflé dish. To prevent top of soufflé from browning further, cut a sheet of aluminum foil large enough to cover top of soufflé. Lightly butter foil and place loosely, buttered side down, over top of soufflé.

Don't make a tight cover or soufflé will not have space to rise again. Bake 30 minutes, or until soufflé has risen. Remove from oven, and this time, serve immediately.

Freezer Chocolate Soufflé   SERVES 8

  3½ ounces semisweet chocolate, coarsely chopped
  6 tablespoons all-purpose flour
  ⅓ cup sugar
  1½ cups light cream, divided
  1 tablespoon strong black coffee
  2 teaspoons vanilla
  2 tablespoons butter, softened
  5 egg yolks
  7 egg whites
  ¾ teaspoon cream of tartar
  2 tablespoons confectioners sugar

Put chocolate in top of double boiler over (not in) simmering water. Stir until melted. Remove from heat and set aside to cool. Place flour, sugar, and ¾ cup cream in medium-size saucepan, mix well, and cook over low heat, stirring constantly until smooth. Add remaining ¾ cup cream and bring mixture to a boil, stirring constantly. Remove from heat and beat in melted chocolate, coffee, vanilla, and butter. Scrape mixture into mixing bowl. Beat egg yolks and add to chocolate mixture all at once. Beat until well combined. Beat egg whites with cream of tartar until soft peaks form. Add confectioners sugar and continue beating until stiff peaks form. Stir 2 heaping tablespoonfuls of beaten egg whites into chocolate mixture. Fold in remaining egg whites. Line a 2-quart soufflé dish with aluminum foil, using enough foil to extend 2 to 3 inches above rim of dish. Spoon mixture into foil-lined dish, cover, and freeze until solid. When firm, grasp foil containing frozen soufflé and remove from dish. Wrap soufflé tightly and place in large plastic bag. Store in freezer up to one month. To bake: Preheat oven to 350° F. Butter a 2-quart soufflé dish and sprinkle buttered surface with sugar. Turn dish upside down and tap lightly to remove excess sugar. Make a collar, 2 inches high, butter and sugar inside of collar and wrap it around soufflé dish. Remove soufflé from freezer, unwrap and place in prepared dish. Let stand at room temperature 1 hour. Bake soufflé 1 hour and 10 minutes until puffed (center will shake gently). Serve at once with chocolate sauce or sweetened whipped cream.

NICE TO KNOW: Sprinkle top of soufflé with confectioners sugar during last 10 minutes of baking for a shiny sugar glaze.

QUICK SOLUTIONS

Soufflé breaks apart in oven

• Divide into serving portions in kitchen. Top with sauce.

Soufflé deflates before you serve it

• Divide into serving portions in kitchen. Top with sauce.
• If you made a "double-rising" soufflé, return it to oven for further cooking. It will rise again. SERVE IMMEDIATELY.

CHECKLIST FOR NEXT TIME

Problem	Probable Cause
Soufflé browns on top before it has risen properly	– Was oven temperature too high?
Soufflé does not rise properly	– Did you beat egg whites too short a time? – Did you neglect to fold egg whites into soufflé base immediately after you beat them? – Did you stir in egg whites, instead of folding them in properly?
Soufflé falls during baking	– Did you open oven door too often? – Did you slam oven door?
Soufflé breaks apart in oven	– Did you forget to put a collar around the soufflé dish?
Soufflé collapses before serving	– Did you try to hold the soufflé instead of serving it as soon as you removed it from oven?
Soufflé not done in time	– Was oven temperature too low?

TEMPERATURE

Although you may not realize it, temperature can be the cause of more disasters in the kitchen than almost any other single factor. My friends, colleagues, and students all view me as something of a thermometer freak. I have a whole collection of kitchen thermometers—and I use every one of them.

When was the last time you checked the temperature inside your oven? If it is wrong, you can ruin the food you are cooking. You should have a good oven thermometer and use it to check your oven regularly. Set the oven at 350° F. and if the thermometer tells you the temperature is off, you can make the necessary adjustment by setting the oven higher or lower. Then, the next time you have an appliance repair person in the house, ask him to calibrate the oven. He should be able to do it in about fifteen minutes, and if he is repairing something else at the same time, he may not even charge for the service.

But oven thermostats are not always entirely dependable. Even if you have your oven calibrated regularly, you still should keep a constant check on the internal temperature. Unfortunately, some oven thermometers are not as reliable as they should be either. If you are serious about cooking at the correct temperature, invest in a mercury thermometer, and replace it periodically. It won't work properly forever.

Other appliances should have their temperatures taken, too. A refrigerator must be kept at 36° F. to 40° F. For a freezer the correct temperature is between 0° F. and −10° F. If these temperatures are not properly maintained, the quality of food will be adversely affected, and occasionally the food will spoil. With prices as high as they are these days, having to throw food out is just about the ultimate disaster.

If you don't mind gambling, you can cook meat by the clock or by your gut instincts. But if you really want to be absolutley certain your meat will not be overcooked or undercooked, you need a meat thermometer. There are two kinds. One model is inserted in the meat before it goes into the oven and must be placed so the tip is in the center of the meat and does not touch bone, fat, or gristle. The trouble with this kind of thermometer is that it conducts heat into the center of the meat, which in turn somewhat changes the way the meat cooks. It also allows precious juices to run out.

The other kind, an instant thermometer, will do a better job. It is not left in place while the meat cooks, but is used only at the point you want to check the progress of the meat. This type of thermometer can also be used when meat has been cooked in a microwave oven. Instant thermometers register up to 220° F. and can also be used to check the temperature of water, yeast, dough, sauces, or anything within that temperature range that requires a specific temperature for successful cooking.

Candy and deep-frying thermometers must register up to 400° F. to be of much help. Candy that is not cooked to the correct temperature simply will not turn out as expected or desired. Food that is deep-fried at the wrong temperature will be soggy or burned. Since both candy and deep-fried food are often cooked in batches, you can easily see for yourself the varied results you will get in different batches when you don't monitor temperatures carefully.

If you spend money for the thermometers you ought to have, you will more than cover the cost by what you will save on food that won't have to be thrown away.

TIMING

Even though I have been cooking for many years, there is one meal I am almost never able to time correctly: breakfast. Without an extra set of hands, I find it virtually impossible to get fruit, toast, eggs, bacon, and coffee done at exactly the same moment. I presume the reason I have so much difficulty is because I don't function at full capacity in the morning. Most of the time my breakfast problems are not very important. But timing is vital for the success of dinner, and this takes planning and good organization.

If your menu does not include food that can be prepared ahead of time and held safely without damaging the quality of the food, then you must make what amounts to a backwards timetable. Begin with the time you want to serve the food, estimate the time each dish will take to cook, and count backwards so you know at what time to start cooking each dish. Then estimate the amount of preparation time necessary before cooking can begin.

But there are many other factors that go into good timing. A menu must be planned, for example, around the equipment you have available. If you have only one oven, you can't possibly serve spinach soufflé and broiled lamb chops, and have them ready at the same time. You will run into exactly the same kind of problem if you are using the oven to cook a main dish and you make the mistake of planning to serve an hors d'oeuvre that must be run under the broiler.

If you have the space and funds to install a second oven, your menus can be expanded enormously. But there are other kinds of cooking equipment that also can be helpful. A small portable oven/toaster can take some of the pressure off the use of a bigger oven. Use it to bake a small casserole, keep food warm, heat rolls, or broil small amounts of food. A microwave oven can be used to speed up defrosting when you have forgotten to take something out of the freezer in time. It also can be used to cook many dishes in less time than by traditional means. And you'll find a microwave oven mighty convenient to reheat food that has been cooked ahead of time and has cooled off. Steamers, double boilers, and heat regulators can all be used effectively to keep food warm without overcooking. And of course a pressure cooker can dramatically reduce the time needed to cook any number of foods—a godsend in an emergency.

The real trick in learning how to make everything come out at the same time is to plan a menu that includes some food that can be cooked ahead of time and then held before serving or reheated quickly without watching or spoiling. Don't plan a menu with several dishes that all require last-minute cooking, garnishing, tossing, or saucing. Use a timer to alert you when something needs to be turned off or turned over, and try to include no more than one really elaborate dish in a meal.

If someone is sitting at the breakfast table waiting for eggs and bacon, it is easy enough to ask that person to watch the toast for you. But you probably won't want to invite an assortment of dinner guests into your kitchen to help while you turn the steak, make a béarnaise sauce, drain and season the asparagus, try to figure out where to heat the garlic bread, toss the salad, start the coffee, and unmold and garnish a chocolate bombe.

The key to good timing is careful menu planning.

One aspect of timing I never have seen discussed in a cookbook is the confusing question of how long it really takes to cook specific foods. One cookbook directs the cook to poach a chicken breast for fifteen minutes and another says forty-five minutes. One writer says to sauté a veal cutlet for two or three minutes on each side and the next book says to cook the same meat for thirty minutes. So far as I am able to determine the explanation evidently is related to geography.

In the same way, a specific food may have one name in the Northeast, a second name in the Midwest, and still another name in the South. Customs related to how food is cooked and served also vary from one part of the country to another, and from one nation to another. As a result, cooking times given in a cookbook often relate to where the writer comes from.

Whenever a cook is faced with conflicting instructions on how long a food should be cooked, my recommendation is to cook the food for the shortest time suggested and then check it. You can always cook the food longer. With the exceptions of food that must be cooked to a specific temperature in order to be safe to eat, and of food that must be cooked a specific amount of time in order to rise, thicken, solidify, or crisp, the length of time most food can be cooked is often a matter of preference. If you are used to cooking food for a very long time, you may find you can save time—and energy, too—by shortening the process. Food is more nourishing when the nutrients are not cooked out, and it has more flavor as well.

Next time you see a recipe where logic tells you the cooking time probably can be reduced, experiment. You may be correct. There simply is no reason why, for example, a casserole that consists primarily of precooked food must be baked in an oven for forty-five minutes to an hour. If it looks hot and bubbly after twenty minutes, don't be a slave to a poorly written cookbook. Throw the book away, take the food out of the oven, and enjoy it.

VEGETABLES

One almost infallible way to make an immediate judgment about the quality of food served in a restaurant is to taste the vegetables. If they are overcooked and waterlogged (or worse yet, canned), you can be reasonably certain the quality of all the food served will be less than exciting. Although vegetables are among the easiest kinds of food to cook, they are poorly cooked more often than almost any other food, in restaurants and in homes.

There are many ways to cook vegetables, and in the long run, the most accepted way is often the least satisfactory. Most of the time, vegetables are cooked in lightly salted boiling water. Overcooking occurs more often when they are cooked this way than by almost any other method. Even when the heat is turned off at just the right moment, vegetables go right on cooking if they are allowed to remain in the hot water. By the time you are ready to serve them, they are overcooked. In addition, if they are not drained very thoroughly, they end up sitting in a very unappetizing puddle. Insufficient draining will dilute any sauce you might add and will contribute to the general soggy appearance of the vegetables.

Some vegetables can be cooked successfully in a skillet with butter or margarine without ever seeing the inside of a pot of boiling water. It is still important not to overcook them, but no matter what you do, they won't get waterlogged. Sliced carrots, zucchini, or yellow squash are examples of vegetables that can be sautéed very successfully.

Most vegetables that can be boiled can also be steamed. A steamed vegetable cannot possibly get waterlogged and it never needs to be drained. But if you steam vegetables too long, they can also be over-cooked. A steamer is a readily available, inexpensive piece of cooking equipment that can be used to cook food and, when necessary, keep food warm. When you steam vegetables, you have the added advan-tage of not losing valuable nutrients that are in the cooking water and are invariably wasted if you don't save the pot liquor. You will also find that steamed green vegetables turn a magnificent deep green color and are more attractive than boiled vegetables.

I find that vegetables taste best when they are served slightly crunchy, rather than very soft. When vegetables are cooked beyond the soft state and are hopelessly overcooked, you can still use them in a variety of ways. If you are almost ready to serve dinner and you don't have time to cook another vegetable, place them in the blender or food processor and puree them. Enrich the puree with butter and cream, season well, and serve as though you had intended to serve a pureed vegetable all along. Although most of us would insist we usually don't serve vegetables that have been pureed, the fact is that anyone who serves mashed potatoes or turnips, or even pumpkin pie, has served a pureed vegetable. Cranberry sauce, apple sauce, and even tomato sauce are all examples of popular and familiar pureed foods. Use the recipe that follows as a model. This is the way many vegetables are served in elegant restaurants.

Puree of Carrots   SERVES 6

1½ **pounds overcooked carrots**
  5 **tablespoons butter, melted**
  2 **tablespoons brown sugar**
     Salt and freshly ground pepper to taste
¾ **to 1 cup heavy cream**
  2 **tablespoons freshly chopped chives or parsley**
¼ **cup finely chopped walnuts (optional)**

Drain carrots well. Place in a heavy saucepan over moderate heat and shake pan gently 1 to 2 minutes to remove excess moisture. Place half the carrots and half the butter in container of food processor or blender and process until smooth. Remove to saucepan. Process remaining carrots and butter and add to saucepan. (You should have approximately 2 cups of puree.) Add sugar, salt, and pepper. Place over low heat. Gradually pour in cream, stirring constantly, until all ingredients are well blended. Do not let mixture come to a boil. Remove pan from heat, stir in chives. Place in serving dish and sprinkle top with walnuts.

NOTE: If puree needs thickening, add 1 or 2 beaten egg yolks and blend well.

Overcooked vegetables can also be turned into a creamed soup. If you start out to make a creamed soup, you have to puree a vegetable. So if you puree overcooked vegetables in the blender or food processor and follow the recipe below, you can make a genuinely delicious soup. Then, replace the overcooked vegetable on your menu with a crisp salad or sliced tomatoes, because, if you are serving vegetable soup to start the meal, you don't absolutely have to serve a cooked vegetable with the main course.

Basic Creamed Soup Recipe   SERVES 4

2 tablespoons butter
2 tablespoons all-purpose flour
2 cups milk or 1 cup milk and 1 cup stock
Salt and freshly ground pepper to taste
1½ to 2 cups pureed vegetable
1 cup heavy cream

Melt butter in large, heavy saucepan. Add flour and stir to form smooth paste. Cook 1 to 2 minutes, stirring constantly. Remove from heat and gradually pour in milk, stirring constantly. Return pan to moderate heat and cook until smooth and thickened, stirring constantly. Add pureed vegetable, salt, and pepper, and stir well. Cook until heated through. Place cream in small bowl and add ¼ cup hot soup mixture. Stir until well combined, then pour mixture back into hot soup. Lower heat and cook until soup is heated through. Do not let it come to a boil. Garnish in one of the following ways:

Enrich with 2 tablespoons butter cut into small pieces. Add to soup, one piece at a time, just before serving. This will give soup a gloss. Stir well.

Pale-colored soup is enhanced by garnishes that are crisp in texture and add color. Use strips of raw vegetables, such as red or green pepper, carrots, celery, zucchini, or cucumber. Add just before serving.

Float thin slices of lemon, mushrooms, or cucumber on top of soup.

Add a dollop of sour cream or swirl in 2 tablespoons of heavy cream. Sprinkle with paprika, chopped chives, or parsley.

Top soup with seasoned croutons or slivers of toasted almonds.

For additional flavoring, sauté ¼ cup of diced vegetables, such as onion, garlic, green pepper, or celery, in the butter before you add the flour.

NOTE: If you use a starchy vegetable like potatoes, omit the flour.

Pureed vegetables can be used as topping for a casserole or combined with other food as an extender. If you don't want to use a pureed vegetable immediately, you can use it another time as baby food, as geriatric food, or as a thickener for sauce or gravy. And of course you can always freeze it to use as a pureed vegetable or creamed soup at another meal. The important thing to remember is that if you overcook vegetables you don't have to pour them unaltered into a serving dish and offer them with a brave smile—and you don't have to throw them away, either.

QUICK SOLUTIONS

Vegetables are overcooked

- Puree:
    season and serve as an elegant side dish;
    use as the base for a creamed soup;
    use as thickener in a gravy or sauce.

Vegetables are undercooked

- (This is rarely a problem since many vegetables are delicious raw or partially cooked.) To speed cooking, chop partially cooked vegetables into smaller pieces and continue cooking.

Vegetables lack flavor

- Add butter, herbs, spices, and/or lemon juice.

Vegetables look faded or unappetizing

• Garnish with paprika, freshly chopped greens, browned bread crumbs, toasted slivered almonds, or grated cheese.

Part of vegetable seems tough and woody

• Cut off tough stems and discard. Continue to cook remaining vegetables if necessary.

CHECKLIST FOR NEXT TIME

Problem	Probable Cause
Vegetables are overcooked	– Did you let them stand in hot water after they were fully cooked? – Did you forget to check them periodically while they were cooking?
Vegetables are tough	– Did you forget to trim them adequately before cooking? – Did you start with vegetables that were too mature?
Vegetables are soggy	– Did you let them stand in hot water after they were fully cooked? – Did you forget to drain them thoroughly before adding butter and seasoning?
Vegetables lack flavor or color	– Did you cook them in too much water? – Did you cook them too long?

WEATHER

Even when you choose a reliable recipe, use exactly the ingredients specified, and follow all the instructions precisely, a recipe still can fail. As a matter of fact, a recipe you have made successfully in the past can fail miserably, too. This is because some foods are seriously affected by the weather. And that's why it is important to know what you can't do in the kitchen under certain weather conditions, even if it means making last-minute changes in a menu.

Most candy, particularly chocolate, nougats, fondants, hard candy, and divinity, must be made in a room in which the temperature is between 60° F. and 68° F. The humidity must be low, and the cooking area should be free from drafts and from the hot vapors of other foods being prepared. Don't try to make candy on a hot humid day. It will not set and you will end up with a sticky mess.

A rainy day is not the day to make jam or jelly either. It simply will not gel. Even if it is not quite raining, but the humidity is high, your jams and jellies still may not set, or the setting may be retarded so severely that it might well be two or three days before you can determine whether or not they are ever going to gel.

Baked goods that contain yeast are also affected by high humidity. The dough will rise too fast and lose its elasticity, gluten will react too quickly with the yeast, and the dough will be difficult to knead. Pick a spot for yeast dough to rise where the temperature is between 75° F. to 80° F. If the area is too cold, the dough will not rise as quickly as it should. If the area is too hot, the dough will rise too rapidly. When you place bread on a rack to cool, keep it away from drafts. A draft will cause the bread to shrink.

Meringues cooked during damp, humid weather will be soggy and will deflate. Keep meringues that are not going to be used immediately in airtight containers to prevent them from absorbing moisture from the air and getting gummy or collapsing.

Puff pastry should only be made on a dry, cold day. If you make it in a warm room, the butter will melt and the dough will be greasy. If the weather is hot, and your kitchen is not air conditioned, place an electric fan in the kitchen to circulate air while you work. But don't allow air to blow directly on the work surface or on the pastry.

Crème fraiche requires a warm atmosphere. The colder the atmosphere, the longer it will take for *crème fraiche* to reach the correct consistency.

Mayonnaise is especially temperamental. It cannot be made during a thunderstorm. Even if a storm is just on the way, the mayonnaise will not thicken. And if the temperature and/or humidity are very high when you're making mayonnaise, be prepared for a greasy dressing.

Recipes that call for cooked sugar mixtures cannot be made successfully on a rainy day. Therefore, in addition to jams and jellies, something like a French lace cookie will also be a disaster if you don't wait for the sun to come out.

Cakes, cookies, cereal products, crackers, potato chips, and similar foods suffer from humidity much as humans do. They all become limp and soggy. To keep them as fresh as possible, store them in airtight containers. Many of these and other foods can be crisped in the oven, unless of course it is so hot that the last thing in the world you want to do is turn on the oven. They cannot be crisped in a microwave oven.

When a tried and trusted recipe fails and you can't think of any logical reason why, look out the window. The answer to your question may be in the heavens.

WHIPPED CREAM

Whipped cream can be used to dress up a dessert or even a cup of coffee. It can, of course, be made at the last minute—although it doesn't have to be. I love my food processor and use it whenever I can, but I do not recommend it for whipping cream. It is not possible to make properly whipped cream in most food processors because their design does not allow enough air to be incorporated into the cream.

It's necessary to chill the bowl and beaters in advance to be sure heavy cream will not start to turn while you are whipping it. To flavor whipped cream, add the confectioners sugar, vanilla, brandy, instant coffee, or whatever you want, after the cream has begun to thicken. If you add flavoring too soon, the cream may never thicken properly. If you add it too late, the additional beating may cause the cream to start turning to butter.

I have seen a variety of suggestions for rescuing overwhipped cream, but I don't think any of them really works very well. Once the cream has begun to turn to butter, there is no way to eliminate the grainy texture or slightly buttery taste. It is better to keep going and actually make butter. The quickest way to do that is to put your over-whipped cream in a food processor, add about one-half cup of chipped ice and process until you have very watery butter. Drain it thoroughly and use it as you would use butter. It is delicious. Expensive, but still delicious.

If you are concerned that your heavy cream may not be as fresh as it should be, add one-eighth teaspoon of baking soda for each cup of cream before you start to whip. This should prevent the cream from curdling.

When you want to whip cream several hours in advance or plan to pipe whipped cream through a pastry bag, it needs extra body. You can provide it by softening one-half teaspoon of unflavored gelatin in two teaspoons of cold water. Scald one-fourth cup of cream and add it to the gelatin mixture. Stir until the gelatin is completely dissolved. Refrigerate this mixture until it is thoroughly chilled, but not set (about twenty minutes). Whip the remaining three-fourths cup of cream and, before it is fully whipped, add the chilled gelatin mixture and finish whipping. Gelatin-stabilized cream will not separate or get runny and it will hold its shape for as many days as the cream remains fresh.

Should you need to stretch or lighten whipped cream, you can fold in a stiffly beaten egg white. This will make the cream go further, but it will not be firm enough to pipe.

In the event that you don't have any heavy cream on hand, you can whip either evaporated milk or nonfat dry milk instead. Neither is as stable or delicious as heavy cream but they can be flavored in the same way as heavy cream is flavored.

To whip evaporated milk, refrigerate undiluted evaporated milk for several hours or place it in the freezer until tiny ice crystals form. Whip it in the same way you would whip heavy cream. You can stabilize it to some degree by adding gelatin or by folding in two tablespoons of either lemon juice or vinegar for each cup of milk, after the milk has been whipped.

If you want to use nonfat dry milk, combine one-half cup of the dry milk with one-third cup of water, mix well, and chill in the refrigerator. Whip until slightly thickened. Add one tablespoon of lemon juice and continue whipping.

WHEN
ALL ELSE
FAILS

Food—and recipes—for almost any emergency

Every cook should have a few special, fail-proof "company" recipes to fall back on in an emergency. Cooking failures certainly create unexpected emergencies, but unanticipated company can also cause big problems. Having recipes you can use in an emergency is only half the solution. You must also have on hand the ingredients called for in those recipes.

Everyone has a list of basic staples to be bought almost automatically and kept on hand. The foods included in that list provide a fascinating picture of a family's eating habits, once you go beyond such basic food as flour and sugar. In one household it may be a disaster to run out of fresh coffee. In the next household, really fine tea is a must. Some kitchens are always stocked with fresh garlic, freshly ground Parmesan cheese, and homemade stock, while other kitchens have shelves full of convenience foods and a good supply of frankfurters. The supplies kept on hand reflect many things: the time available for cooking, and skill and experience of the cook, the ages of the members of the household, and their preferences in food.

The list of ingredients that follows includes food that can be kept on hand (for a reasonable time) without spoiling and can be used when circumstances create the need for quick, easy company fare. Many items on the list are fine ingredients that can be used without apology at any time. Others are by no means as good as the fresh foods they are substitutes for, but you will be glad to have them in a pinch.

In the pantry:

ANCHOVY FILLETS: for quick appetizers; dress up salads; add to casseroles
ANCHOVY PASTE: flavor appetizers and sauces
ARROWROOT OR CORNSTARCH: thicken sauces and gravy·
ARTICHOKE HEARTS (canned): dress up salads
ASPARAGUS (canned): add to casseroles
BEAN SPROUTS (canned): add to salads and stir-fry recipes
BISCUIT MIX: for quick biscuits, dumplings, and casserole toppings
BOUILLON, BOTH BEEF AND CHICKEN (cubes or canned): use in place of
   homemade stock
BROWNIE MIX: quick desserts
BROWNING SAUCE: add color to gravy
CAKE MIXES: quick desserts
CAPERS: dress up chicken or shrimp salads; add to steak tartare; use in sauces
CHOCOLATE AND COCOA: flavor cakes; make emergency toppings
CORNSTARCH: special thickening agent
CORN SYRUP: for flavoring
CRANBERRY SAUCE: use as accompaniment to main dishes; as flavoring
   agent in sauces and gelatin molds
CLAMS, MINCED (canned): for appetizers, quick clam sauce; add to salads
   and casseroles
CLAMS, WHOLE (canned): for chowders
CONFECTIONERS SUGAR: for quick icings
CORNMEAL: for biscuits and bread
CRAB MEAT (canned): for appetizers and casseroles
CREAMED SOUP (canned): for soup bases, sauces, and casseroles
CROUTONS: dress up salads; casserole toppings
EVAPORATED MILK: make emergency whipped topping
FRUIT (canned): quick desserts; dress up salads; garnish for main dishes
GARLIC (fresh): for flavor
GELATIN: make molds; stabilize whipped cream
HERBS AND SPICES: for flavoring
HONEY: for flavoring
HOT PEPPER SAUCE: for flavoring
MELBA TOAST: for quick appetizers
MUSHROOMS (canned): to dress up vegetables and casseroles
MUSTARD, dry and good quality prepared: for flavoring
OLIVE OIL: in salad dressings; for sautéing
OLIVES: for garnishing
ONION SOUP MIX: make quick dips; flavor sauces
PAPRIKA, imported: for flavoring and color
PASTA: for quick casseroles and side dishes
PEANUT BUTTER: soup; flavor sauce

PEAS, tiny (canned): for main dishes, casseroles, and emergency side dishes
PIMIENTO: for garnishing
PRESERVES: for sauces and flavoring
PUDDING MIXES: quick desserts
RICE: for quick side dishes or casseroles
SHERRY, dry: for flavoring soup and main dishes
SHRIMP (canned): for appetizers, salads, and main dishes
SOY SAUCE: as flavoring agent
TOMATOES, stewed, paste, sauce (canned): for sauce bases and casseroles
VERMOUTH, dry: for flavoring; use as stable substitute for white wine
VINEGAR, top quality: for salad dressings
WATER CHESTNUTS: in appetizers and main dishes
WORCESTERSHIRE SAUCE: for sauce, gravies, flavoring

In the refrigerator (limited safe storage):

BACON: in appetizers, salads, and main dishes
CELERY: flavoring soup, casseroles, and sauces; quick appetizers
CHEESES, including cream cheese: for appetizers; for dessert; as a topping; for
   flavoring sauces
CREAM, including dairy sour cream: for sauces and desserts
GARLIC, minced in soy sauce: to flavor salad dressings, sauces, and
   main dishes
HORSERADISH (prepared): for flavoring
JALAPENO RELISH: to flavor appetizers and sauces
LEMONS: for flavoring: for garnishing
MAYONNAISE: for appetizers, salad dressings, and sauces
PARSLEY: for flavoring; for garnishing

In the freezer:

ARTICHOKE HEARTS: for appetizers; add to casseroles
ASPARAGUS: add to casseroles
BERRIES: serve as dessert; make quick sauces
CHICKEN, cutlets, broilers, and livers: for appetizers, salads, and main dishes
CHIVES, chopped: for flavoring and garnishing
COCKTAIL RYE OR PUMPERNICKEL: for quick appetizers
COCONUT: use in desserts and ethnic main dishes
CRAB MEAT: for appetizers and main dishes
CRANBERRIES: quick side dish
FRUIT: serve as dessert; garnish main dishes; make sauces
GROUND MEAT, lean: emegency appetizers and main dishes
ICE CREAM, various flavors: serve as dessert
NUTS: add to appetizers, main dishes, salads, and desserts
PARMESAN CHEESE, grated: add to sauces; use in or on main dishes

PATTY SHELLS: fill with main dish recipes; fill for dessert
PHYLLO DOUGH: fill for appetizers, main dishes, and desserts
PIE CRUSTS: quick appetizers, light dishes, and desserts
PUFF PASTRY: make appetizers, main dishes, and desserts
ROLLS, PARTY: filler at lunch or with dinner
SHRIMP: for main dishes, quick salads, appetizers
SOUP: quick sauces; use in casseroles
STOCK: for soup or sauce bases; use in main dishes
VEGETABLES: use in casseroles

Quick Clam Puff   SERVES 6 TO 8

1 package (8 ounces) cream cheese, softened
½ cup mayonnaise
1 small onion, grated
1 can (6½ ounces) minced clams, drained
2 tablespoons finely chopped pimientos, well drained
1 tablespoon chopped chives (optional)
2 teaspoons Worcestershire sauce
Hot pepper sauce to taste

Preheat oven to 375° F. Mash cream cheese with fork. Add remaining ingredients and stir until well combined. Spoon into 1-quart baking dish and bake 20 to 25 minutes, or until top is lightly browned and slightly puffy. Serve hot with melba rounds or crackers.

If you want to make individual hors d'oeuvre, prepare a package of frozen artichoke hearts according to package directions. Drain well and spoon heaping teaspoon of clam mixture on top of each artichoke half. Place under broiler and cook until puffed and lightly browned. Serve hot.

This recipe is also delicious served cold as a dip. Combine all ingredients and place in serving bowl. Cover and refrigerate at least 1 hour. Serve with crisp vegetables, crackers, or party rye bread.

ALTERNATE METHOD: Instead of using softened cream cheese, you can process cheese straight from the refrigerator in food processor until smooth. Add remaining ingredients, process, and proceed as directed above.

Hot Cheese Canapes   ABOUT 18 APPETIZERS

    4 tablespoons butter, softened
    1 cup shredded extra sharp Cheddar cheese
    1 medium-size onion, grated
    2 tablespoons mayonnaise
    2 tablespoons jalapeño relish, drained
      Hot pepper sauce to taste
      Cocktail rye or pumpernickel

Combine butter, cheese, onion, mayonnaise, relish, and hot pepper sauce.
Spread on slices of cocktail bread and broil until cheese is slightly melted and
piping hot. Serve immediately.

Horseradish Dip   ABOUT 1½ CUPS

    1 package (8 ounces) cream cheese
    ½ cup dairy sour cream
    3 to 4 tablespoons freshly grated horseradish or 1 bottle
      (6 ounces) prepared horseradish, well drained
      Hot pepper sauce and salt to taste
      Paprika

Place cream cheese, sour cream, horseradish, hot pepper sauce, and salt in
container of food processor or blender and process until well combined.
Spoon into bowl, garnish wth paprika, and serve with cocktail rye or pumpernickel.

Shrimp Dip   ABOUT 3 CUPS

    1 can (10 ounces) frozen condensed cream of shrimp soup
    1 can (4½ ounces) tiny shrimp, drained
    1 package (3 ounces) cream cheese
    1 to 2 tablespoons lemon juice
    1 to 2 cloves garlic, minced
      Salt and pepper to taste
      Paprika
      Freshly chopped parsley

Place all ingredients in container of blender or food processor until smooth,
but not pureed. Spoon into serving bowl and sprinkle with paprika or chopped
parsley. Serve with melba rounds.

Sherried Asparagus Soup   SERVES 6 TO 8

1 package (10 ounces) frozen asparagus cuts and tips, thawed;
   or 1 can (14½ ounces) asparagus cuts and tips, drained;
   or 2 cups cooked, leftover asparagus, divided
2 cans (10½ ounces each) condensed cream of asparagus soup, divided
2 cups light cream or half and half
1 tablespoon Worcestershire sauce
   Salt and pepper to taste
¼ cup dry sherry
⅓ cup heavy cream
2 hard-cooked egg yolks, sieved, for garnish

Chop asparagus into small pieces. Place 1 can of soup and half the chopped asparagus in blender or food processor and process until smooth. Remove to saucepan. Add remaining can of soup, remaining chopped asparagus, light cream, Worcestershire, salt, and pepper, and heat until just bubbly. Remove from heat and stir in sherry. Ladle into individual bowls. Top each bowl with 1 tablespoon heavy cream swirled through. Sprinkle with sieved eggs.

ANOTHER WAY: Try the same recipe using cream of potato soup and leftover boiled potatoes. Sprinkle with paprika, chopped chives, or scallions.

Goober Soup   SERVES 6

1 medium-size onion, finely chopped
2 tablespoons butter
1 tablespoon all-purpose flour
1 cup peanut butter (smooth or chunky)
2 cans (15¾ ounces each) chicken broth
¼ teaspoon nutmeg
¼ teaspoon ginger
   Salt and pepper to taste
6 tablespoons heavy cream
⅓ cup chopped unsalted peanuts

Sauté onion in butter until onion is transparent. Add flour, stir, and cook 1 minute. Add peanut butter and stir to combine. Add broth slowly, stirring constantly. Season with nutmeg, ginger, salt, and pepper and cook over moderate heat until thoroughly warmed, about 15 minutes.

Icy Blueberry Soup   SERVES 4

1 package (16 ounces) frozen blueberries
½ cup sugar
Juice of 1 lemon
1 stick cinnamon or 2 teaspoons cinnamon
Pinch of salt
2 cups dairy sour cream or plain yogurt

Place blueberries in large saucepan with 3 cups cold water, sugar, lemon juice, cinnamon stick, and salt. Bring mixture to a boil, lower heat, cover, and simmer about 10 minutes. Remove cinnamon stick and press mixture through sieve or puree in 2 batches in food processor. Pour into large bowl, cover, and refrigerate until well chilled. To serve, remove from refrigerator and stir into sour cream. Ladle into soup bowls and garnish with additional blueberries (if you have them), sour cream, or a thin slice of lemon.

New England Clam Chowder   SERVES 6 TO 8

4 medium-size potatoes, peeled and diced
4 slices bacon, cut into small pieces
   (salt pork may be substituted)
1 medium-size onion, finely chopped
2 cans (10 ounces each) whole baby clams, undrained
3 cups milk
1 cup heavy cream
   Salt and freshly ground pepper to taste
2 to 3 tablespoons butter
   Fresh chopped parsley to garnish

Place potatoes in a saucepan, cover with lightly salted water, and cook gently about 15 minutes until just tender. Drain and set aside. Fry bacon in medium-size skillet until crisp. Drain on paper towel. Set aside. Sauté onion in 4 tablespoons drippings (or butter) until transparent. Add potatoes to skillet and cook over moderate heat about 2 minutes, tossing gently. Transfer onion and potatoes to large saucepan or stock pot; add undrained clams, milk, and cream. Season with salt and pepper and simmer (do not boil) about 10 minutes until very hot. Add bacon bits. Spoon into bowls, top with dot of butter, and garnish with chopped parsley. Serve with oysterettes or biscuits.

NICE TO KNOW: If you prefer a chowder with a stronger clam flavor, substitute 1 cup of clam broth for 1 cup of milk. If you prefer a richer chowder, use more cream and less milk. You can, if necessary, substitute minced clams for whole clams, and of course you can use fresh clams if you have them available.

Turkey Mornay   SERVES 4 TO 6

1 bunch fresh broccoli
8 to 10 slices of cooked turkey breast
4 tablespoons butter
3 tablespoons all-purpose flour
1 cup chicken broth
1 cup half and half
1 egg yolk
3 tablespoons heavy cream
2 teaspoons Worcestershire sauce
Salt and freshly ground pepper to taste
¼ cup dry sherry or vermouth
½ cup grated Parmesan cheese, divided
¼ cup grated Swiss or Gruyere cheese
Freshly grated nutmeg to taste
Cayenne to taste

Steam broccoli or cook in boiling, salted water until crisp-tender. Drain and slice lengthwise. Arrange in bottom of shallow baking dish. Place turkey slices over broccoli. Preheat oven to 400° F. Melt butter in heavy saucepan, add flour, and stir to form smooth paste. Cook roux 2 minutes, stirring constantly. Remove saucepan from heat and gradually pour in broth and half and half, stirring constantly. Return saucepan to low heat and cook, stirring constantly, until thickened and bubbly. Beat egg yolk and cream together. Spoon 3 tablespoons of hot sauce into egg-cream mixture, stir well, and pour into hot sauce. Add Worcestershire, salt, pepper, sherry, ¼ cup Parmesan cheese, Swiss cheese, nutmeg, and cayenne. Cook over low heat until cheese is melted, stirring constantly. Pour sauce over turkey, covering completely. Sprinkle top with remaining ¼ cup Parmesan cheese. Place in oven and bake 20 minutes, or until top is lightly browned and bubbly.

ALTERNATE METHODS: You can prepare this dish with cooked, sliced chicken breasts instead of turkey. You can also substitute frozen broccoli or asparagus for fresh broccoli. If fresh asparagus is in season, use 1½ pounds.

If you happen to have crepes in your freezer, and the only meat you have on hand is boiled ham, try this variation: Place one slice of ham on top of each crepe. Place cooked broccoli stalk or 2 asparagus spears on top of each slice of ham. Roll up jelly-roll style and place in shallow baking dish. Make sauce as directed and pour over filled crepes. Bake as directed.

Company Tetrazzini   SERVES 6

2 tablespoons butter
1 medium-size onion, chopped
2 cans (10¾ ounces each) cream of mushroom soup, undiluted*
1 cup heavy cream
¼ cup dry white wine or sherry
¾ cup grated Parmesan cheese, divided
1 jar (2 ounces) chopped pimiento, drained
½ pound thin spaghetti, cooked al dente
1½ cups cooked, cubed chicken
   Freshly chopped parsley

Preheat oven to 375° F. Melt butter in saucepan and sauté onion until transparent. Add soup and cream and stir well. Cook over low heat about 3 minutes. Stir in wine, half the cheese, and pimiento. Combine spaghetti and chicken in large casserole. Pour sauce over and mix well. Top with remaining cheese and bake in preheated oven 15 to 20 minutes or until hot and bubbly. Garnish with chopped parsley.

*When time permits, substitute 1 pound fresh sliced mushrooms and 3½ cups béchamel sauce for the mushroom soup and cream. You can also vary this dish by substituting cooked, cubed turkey or ham for the chicken. Just add a salad and crusty French bread for a complete meal.

Quick Creamed Shrimp   SERVES 6

1 package (10 ounces) frozen patty shells
1 package (16 ounces) cleaned, deveined frozen shrimp
3 tablespoons all-purpose flour
3 tablespoons butter
1 cup milk
½ cup dry white wine
1 can (4 ounces) sliced mushrooms, drained
1 can (8½ ounces) tiny peas
1 jar (2 ounces) finely chopped pimiento, drained
2 teaspoons Worcestershire sauce
   Hot pepper sauce to taste

Preheat oven and prepare patty shells according to package directions. Keep warm. Prepare shrimp according to package directions, drain and set aside. Melt butter in medium-size saucepan, add flour, and stir to form a smooth paste. Cook roux 2 minutes, stirring constantly. Remove from heat, gradually pour in milk, stirring constantly. Return to medium heat, add Worcestershire and hot pepper sauce, and cook until thickened and bubbly, stirring constantly. Add wine, mushrooms, peas, and reserved shrimp. Cook 3 minutes or until heated through. Remove from heat and stir in pimiento. Spoon into hollowed out patty shells and serve with a crisp green salad and crusty French bread.

If you don't have frozen patty shells in your freezer, use cream puffs instead. They are easy to make, particularly if you own a food processor.

Easy Cream Puffs   MAKES ABOUT 15

> ½ **cup butter**
> ¼ **teaspoon salt**
> 1 **cup sifted all-purpose flour**
> 4 **eggs**

Combine 1 cup water, butter, and salt in saucepan and bring to a boil. Remove from heat and add flour all at once. Stir vigorously until mixture forms a ball and comes away from sides of saucepan. Let stand 5 minutes. Preheat oven to 375° F. Place dough in container of food processor and add eggs, 1 at a time, processing after each addition until smooth and well blended. Drop 2 large rounded tablespoons of dough onto ungreased cookie sheets, spacing cream puffs 2 to 3 inches apart. Bake 15 minutes, lower heat to 350° F., and bake 15 to 20 minutes longer, or until golden brown. Carefully cut off tops, and pull out centers. Let cool on rack 5 minutes, then fill.

ALTERNATE METHOD: Follow instructions above but add eggs to mixture in saucepan 1 at a time. Beat vigorously with wooden spoon after each egg is added until is it thoroughly incorporated. Continue as directed.

Cream puffs can also be used to make a quick emergency dessert. Add 2 tablespoons sugar to batter before adding eggs. Follow procedures above and fill with flavored whipped cream or ice cream. Top with Hot Fudge Sauce Supreme, page 28.

Chicken Livers in Puff Pastry   SERVES 6

1 package (10 ounces) frozen patty shells
1 pound chicken livers, cut into chunks
2 tablespoons butter
1 medium-size onion, chopped
½ pound mushrooms, finely chopped
  Salt and pepper to taste
1½ tablespoons all-purpose flour
1 cup chicken stock or broth
¼ cup brandy or dry vermouth
  Freshly chopped parsley

Bake patty shells according to package directions. Sauté chicken livers in butter about 5 minutes. Add onion, mushrooms, salt, and pepper and cook until onion is transparent. Sprinkle with flour and stir well. Cook 1 minute. Gradually pour in stock and cook, stirring constantly, until slightly thickened. Add ¼ cup brandy and stir. Remove tops from baked patty shells and fill with chicken livers. Garnish with parsley and serve with salad.

NICE TO KNOW: Make the chicken liver filling whenever you have accumulated 1 pound of chicken livers in the freezer. Freeze the cooked mixture and keep it on hand in the freezer so all you have to do is bake the shells and defrost and heat the filling when unexpected company appears.

Crab Newburg   SERVES 6

2 packages (6 ounces each) frozen king crab meat, thawed
4 tablespoons butter
½ cup dry sherry
¼ teaspoon nutmeg
  Dash thyme
½ teaspoon paprika
3 egg yolks
1 cup heavy cream
  Salt and freshly ground pepper to taste

Thoroughly drain and pick over crab meat. Cut into bite-size pieces and set aside. Melt butter in medium-size saucepan. Add crab meat and sauté 3 minutes. Add sherry, nutmeg. thyme, and paprika and cook over low heat 2 to 3 minutes. Beat egg yolks and cream together and slowly pour into saucepan, stirring constantly. Cook over low heat until thickened (don't let mixture boil). Season with salt and pepper and serve over toast points or rice.

NICE TO KNOW: You can substitute almost any combination of cooked seafood: shrimp, lobster, thick fish fillets, or scallops.

Tarragon-Lemon Chicken   SERVES 4

1 3 to 3½ pound broiler/fryer, split
Lemon juice
Tarragon
Salt, pepper, and paprika

Trim excess fat from chicken. Rinse under cold running water and pat dry with paper towels. Squeeze lemon juice over chicken and sprinkle with tarragon, salt, pepper, and paprika on both sides. Place, skin side down, in broiler and broil approximately 15 minutes on each side, basting occasionally with pan juices. Serve with cranberry sauce, corn bread sticks or hot biscuits, and a crisp salad.

Artichoke and Mushroom Casserole   SERVES 6

2 packages (9 ounces each) frozen artichoke hearts
1 pound mushrooms, sliced
3 tablespoons butter
1 can (10¾ ounces) cream of mushroom soup, undiluted
3 tablespoons dry sherry
Salt and pepper to taste
Parmesan cheese

Preheat oven to 350° F. Cook artichoke hearts according to package directions. Drain and set aside. Sauté mushrooms in butter 5 minutes. Combine with reserved artichoke hearts, soup, sherry, salt, and pepper. Mix well and spoon into 1½-quart casserole. Top with cheese and bake in preheated oven 20 minutes or until hot and bubbly.

Parmesan Creamed Spinach   SERVES 4

1 package (10 ounces) frozen chopped spinach
1 small onion, minced
1 clove garlic, minced
2 tablespoons butter
1 tablespoon all-purpose flour
¼ teaspoon nutmeg
Salt and pepper to taste
½ cup dairy sour cream
2 tablespoons grated Parmesan cheese

Cook spinach according to package directions. Drain thoroughly and set aside. Sauté onion and garlic in butter until onion is transparent. Add flour, stir, and cook 2 minutes. Add reserved spinach, nutmeg, salt, and pepper. Cook over low heat until thickened. Add sour cream and mix well. Cook gently until thoroughly heated. Place in serving dish and sprinkle with Parmesan cheese.

Company Pasta in a Hurry

Pasta is an excellent meal stretcher, particularly when you have to feed more people than you had expected and you have a limited amount of meat on hand. You can also use pasta to make a quick and easy side dish or an extra main dish.

The quickest and easiest way to serve pasta is to cook it *al dente*, drain it, place it in a warm bowl, and toss it with melted butter, salt, pepper, and freshly grated Parmesan cheese. If you want it to be spicy, add a touch of crushed red pepper. Sprinkle the top with freshly chopped parsley and you will have a dish that is as delicious as it is beautiful.

If you want to turn your pasta into fettucini, add 1½ cups of warmed heavy cream for each 8 ounces of pasta and sprinkle with nutmeg. You can, if you like, add fresh parsley, but don't add crushed red pepper to fettucini.

If you have been saving chicken livers in your freezer, this might be a good time to use them. Sauté the chicken livers with an onion (and mushrooms if you have any on hand), and serve them on a bed of cooked spaghetti or noodles.

About the only limitation on the use of pasta is your imagination. You can serve it with just about any sauce you feel like making.

Spaghetti with pesto sauce, for example, is a delightful dish. You can make pesto in the old-fashioned manner with a mortar and pestle, and a lot of energy, or in the modern way with a blender or food processor. You must use fresh basil. However, if you make the sauce omitting the cheese and butter, you can make a large quantity when fresh basil is available and freeze it or keep it on the pantry shelf. It is worth having on hand for emergency use.

Pesto Sauce   ABOUT 2 CUPS

1⅓ cups olive oil (about), divided
3 cups fresh basil leaves
3 cloves garlic, crushed
20 walnut halves
2 tablespoons pine nuts (optional)
1 teaspoon salt
Freshly ground pepper to taste
½ cup grated Parmesan cheese
½ cup grated Locatelli or Romano cheese
¼ cup butter, softened

Blender or food processor method: Place ½ cup olive oil and all other ingredients except cheeses and butter in container of blender or food processor. Process until finely ground. Add remaining oil and process for a few seconds until smooth. If it is too thick, add more oil. Pour mixture in bowl, add cheeses and beat with a wooden spoon until well blended. Add softened butter and beat in. Spoon over cooked pasta and toss lightly.

NICE TO KNOW: If you want to store pesto on the pantry shelf, follow the recipe above, omitting the cheeses and butter. Pour mixture into glass jar with screw top and add enough olive oil to come about ½ inch above the pesto. When you are ready to use it, add cheese and butter. If you want to keep pesto in the freezer, omit the cheeses and butter, spoon it into small jars, seal tightly, and freeze. To use, thaw in refrigerator, then add cheeses and butter. If the pesto is too thick, add a few tablespoons of boiling water.

Walnut Noodles   SERVES 6 TO 8

1 pound medium-width noodles
½ cup butter
1 cup walnut halves
¾ cup grated Parmesan cheese
Salt and freshly ground pepper to taste
3 tablespoons freshly chopped parsley

Cook noodles according to package directions. While noodles are cooking, melt butter over high heat until butter begins to brown. Drain noodles and place on warm serving platter. Pour butter over, add walnuts, cheese, salt and pepper. Toss well and garnish with parsley.

Festive Shrimp Salad   SERVES 4

1½ pounds shrimp, cooked, peeled, and chilled
3 scallions, thinly sliced or ⅓ cup chopped onion
1 tablespoon lemon juice
⅓ cup chopped celery
¼ cup slivered almonds
1 tablespoon capers (optional)
  Salt and freshly ground pepper to taste
¾ cup mayonnaise
¼ cup dairy sour cream
2 tablespoons vinegar
1 teaspoon sugar
2 tablespoons snipped dill
  Lettuce
  Tomato wedges
  Wedges of hard-cooked egg
  Freshly chopped parsley or sprigs of dill for garnish

Cut shrimp into bite-size pieces and place in bowl. Add scallions, lemon juice, celery, almonds, capers, salt, and pepper and toss lightly. Combine mayonnaise, sour cream, vinegar, sugar, and dill. Add to shrimp and mix well. Place on lettuce-lined serving platter and garnish with wedges of tomato, egg, and chopped parsley or sprigs of dill.

Caesar Salad   SERVES 4

1 cup seasoned croutons
4 tablespoons butter
1 large clove garlic
5 tablespoons olive oil
6 anchovy fillets, drained and cut into small pieces
1 head romaine lettuce
2 tablespoons red wine vinegar
1 egg, simmered 1 minute
1 large lemon
⅓ cup freshly grated imported Romano or Parmesan cheese
  Freshly ground pepper

Sauté croutons in butter and set aside. Cut garlic in half lengthwise. Rub large wooden salad bowl thoroughly with cut sides of garlic. Crush remains of garlic and add to olive oil. Mash anchovy fillets in bottom of salad bowl. Break up lettuce and place in bowl. Pour olive oil and vinegar over lettuce and toss lightly. Break egg over lettuce, squeeze juice from lemon over egg, sprinkle with cheese and freshly ground pepper. Toss and top with croutons. Serve immediately.

Fruit-Nut Delight   SERVES 4 TO 6

3 large apples
2 teaspoons lemon juice
½ cup chopped pecans, walnuts or almonds
½ cup all-purpose flour
¾ cup firmly packed brown sugar
½ teaspoon cinnamon
¼ teaspoon nutmeg
⅛ teaspoon ground clove or allspice
4 tablespoons butter

Preheat oven to 350° F. Lightly butter 1½-quart casserole or 9-inch baking dish or pie pan. Peel, core, and slice fruit; sprinkle with lemon juice and place in bottom of prepared pan. Sprinkle chopped nuts over fruit. Combine flour, sugar, cinnamon, nutmeg, and cloves. Cut butter into flour mixture until mixture resembles coarse crumbs. Spread crumbs over fruit and bake in oven 45 to 50 minutes, or until fruit is tender. Serve slightly warm. Top with scoop of vanilla ice cream or whipped cream, if desired.

NICE TO KNOW: You can use almost any fresh fruit you have on hand: peaches, pears, bananas, nectarines. You can also use canned or frozen fruit but you may have to adjust cooking time. It is also possible to substitute coconut or raisins for the nuts.

If you have made a cake for dessert and it is a disaster, convert the cake into crumbs and use those crumbs instead of the flour as a topping. Combine 1 cup of cake crumbs, spices, and butter, omitting the sugar. Sprinkle fruit with cake crumb topping and bake as directed.

Jamie's Chocolate Crispies   36 COOKIES

½ cup sweet butter
1 ounce (1 square) unsweetened baking chocolate
1 egg, beaten
⅔ cup sugar
¾ teaspoon vanilla
⅓ cup all-purpose flour
   Dash salt
⅔ cup chopped nuts (any kind you have on hand)

Lightly grease 10 x 15-inch jelly-roll pan. Preheat oven to 375° F. Melt butter and chocolate in saucepan over very low heat. Remove from heat, add egg, sugar, and vanilla. Stir well. Fold in flour, salt, and nuts until well combined. Spread batter evenly in prepared pan. Bake in preheated oven 12 to 15 minutes. (Don't let edges of cookies burn.) Cut into small squares as soon as you remove pan from oven, remove cookies from pan, and cool on rack.

This is a wonderful emergency recipe. These thin, crisp, delicious cookies can be served with fruit or ice cream to turn a simple dessert into company fare. They freeze very well in a plastic bag and can be thawed in less than 30 minutes.

Frozen Chocolate Mousse   SERVES 4 TO 6

When unexpected company appears, excuse yourself for a few minutes and dash into the kitchen to make this delicious, but simple, dessert. Place it in the freezer and, by the time you are ready for dessert, it will be ready to serve.

  ¼ **cup sugar**
  3 **egg yolks**
  1 **package (6 ounces) semi-sweet chocolate morsels**
    or 1 cup chocolate bits
  2 **tablespoons brandy or chocolate-flavored liqueur**
  2 **cups heavy cream, or 1 can (13 ounces) well-chilled evaporated milk**

Place sugar in small saucepan, pour in ½ cup water, and bring mixture to a boil, stirring constantly. Boil rapidly 4 minutes. Pour into blender or food processor, add chocolate, and process until mixture is smooth. Add egg yolks slowly, add brandy and process until thoroughly combined. Pour into medium-size bowl. Whip cream and fold into chocolate mixture. Spoon into 1-quart mold, cover with plastic wrap, and place in freezer until set.

Coconut Pears in Ginger Sauce   SERVES 4

  1 **can (16 ounces) pear halves**
  ½ to ⅔ **cup shredded coconut**
  1 **tablespoon cornstarch**
  ½ **teaspoon ginger**
  2 **tablespoons sweet sherry**

Drain pears well, reserving syrup. Roll pears in coconut and place, cut side down, in shallow pan. Broil about 3 inches from heat until coconut is browned, about 6 minutes. Combine reserved pear syrup, cornstarch, and ginger in small saucepan. Cook, stirring constantly, until thickened. Stir in sherry. Place pears in individual serving dishes and spoon sauce over.

Crème de Menthe Brownie Pie   SERVES 8

1 package (15½ ounces) fudge brownie mix
1 quart chocolate chip ice cream, softened
¼ cup green crème de menthe
Hot Fudge Sauce Supreme (page 28)

Prepare brownie mix according to package directions, but bake in 9-inch ceramic or glass pie plate in preheated 350° F. oven 25 to 30 minutes. Let cool completely. Place softened ice cream in bowl. Add crème de menthe and swirl through ice cream with a knife. (Don't overmix or you will not get a "swirled effect" in ice cream.) Spread ice cream over brownie pie quickly. Cover loosely with plastic wrap and place in freezer until ice cream is firm. Prepare Hot Fudge Sauce Supreme, place in bowl, and serve with pie.

(No one has to know you used a mix. This is such a rich, chocolaty dessert, your guests will never guess your secret.)

INDEX

Notes